Malte Hinrichsen

Racist Trademarks

RACISM ANALYSIS

edited by Wulf D. Hund

Series A: Studies

Volume 3

LIT

Malte Hinrichsen

Racist Trademarks

Slavery, Orient, Colonialism and Commodity Culture

LIT

Cover: Wulf D. Hund and Stefanie Affeldt
using illustrations from ›Uncle Tom's Cabin‹
by Hammatt Billings (1851) and George Cruikshank (1852)
and an advertising for ›Cream of Wheat‹ (1921)

Bibliographic information published by the Deutsche Nationalbibliothek
The Deutsche Nationalbibliothek lists this publication in the Deutsche Nationalbibliografie; detailed bibliographic data are available in the Internet at http://dnb.d-nb.de.

ISBN 978-3-643-90285-6

A catalogue record for this book is available from the British Library

Klosbachstr. 107
CH-8032 Zürich
Tel. +41 (0) 44-251 75 05
Fax +41 (0) 44-251 75 06
e-Mail: zuerich@lit-verlag.ch
http://www.lit-verlag.ch

LIT VERLAG Dr. W. Hopf
Berlin 2012
Fresnostr. 2
D-48159 Münster
Tel. +49 (0) 2 51-62 03 20
Fax +49 (0) 2 51-23 19 72
E-Mail: lit@lit-verlag.de
http://www.lit-verlag.de

Distribution:
In Germany: LIT Verlag Fresnostr. 2, D-48159 Münster
Tel. +49 (0) 2 51-620 32 22, Fax +49 (0) 2 51-922 60 99,
e-mail: vertrieb@lit-verlag.de

In Austria: Medienlogistik Pichler-ÖBZ, e-mail: mlo@medien-logistik.at
In Switzerland: B + M Buch- und Medienvertrieb, e-mail: order@buch-medien.ch
In the UK: Global Book Marketing, e-mail: mo@centralbooks.com
In North America: International Specialized Book Services
e-mail: orders@isbs.com

Contents

»Je promenai sur moi un regard objectif, découvris ma noirceur, mes caractères ethniques, – et me défoncèrent le tympan, l'anthropophagie, l'arriération mentale, le fétichisme, les tares raciales, les négriers, et surtout, et surtout: ›Y'a bon banania‹«. (Frantz Fanon)[1]

1. Introduction

Identifying the various stereotypes and prejudices he feels himself confronted with as a Caribbean black in a French metropolis, Frantz Fanon is most notably struck by the racist slogan of cereal producer Banania. Referring to the same campaign and its depiction of a grinning Senegalese soldier, the famous négritude poet Léopold Senghor wanted to »destroy the banania laughter on all the walls of France«.[2] In the very same year as Fanon published *Peau noire, masques blanc*, African American writer Ralph Ellison makes the main character of *Invisible Man* lose his composure when seeing a »cast-iron figure of a very black, red-lipped and wide-mouthed Negro«.[3] And even in a 2001 episode of *The Sopranos* it takes just the black face on the Uncle Ben's box of rice to let the Italian American father have a nervous breakdown about the unwelcome racial background of his daughter's boyfriend.[4]

Either fictional or biographic, all these incidents vividly demonstrate how complex histories of racial exclusion are implicitly inscribed in simplistic stereotypes and how popular culture transmits the condensed connotations to both white and black consumers. Focussing on the role of three particular advertising stereotypes in the process of promoting racism, I want to avoid two main inaccuracies inherent to this specific field of research. On the one hand, general exposures of racist images in advertising often neglect specific contexts and individual subtexts of the used stereotypes;[5] on the other hand, isolated treatments of single racial-

1 Frantz Fanon: Peau noire, masques blancs, p. 90. For a translation, see ch. 4 ›Conclusion‹.

2 »Mais je déchirerai les rires banania sur tous les murs de France«, Léopold S. Senghor: Hosties noires.

3 Ralph Ellison: Invisible Man.

4 David Chase: Proshai, Livushka (The Sopranos, season 3, episode 2).

5 This problem can be found in the still valuable contributions to racist advertising in specific countries, such as David Ciarlo: Advertising Empire;

ised campaigns lack applicable conclusions in the ongoing quest for universal patterns of racist discrimination.[6] Whereas agents of the former commonly focus on a discourse that treats racism as just one of its aspects, advocates of the latter fail to broaden the perspective for interdisciplinary insights. Thus, there are few systematic attempts to analyse a specific racial stereotype against the backdrop of its complex development while also examining its multiple implications for contemporary popular culture.[7] On a broader scale, it is especially the few non-English publications, namely Jan Nederveen Pieterse's already translated *White on Black* and Raymond Bachollet et al.'s *Négripub*, that attempt systematic approaches towards the specific historical messages of common patterns of stereotyping.[8] However, the only available extensive corporate histories about Banania and Sarotti, written in French and German, are useful sources for dates and images, but basically lack any critical analysis of their subject and read »like an extended ad« for the respective company.[9]

Most of the significant examinations of race in advertising can be derived from Anne McClintock's prominent spadework of 1995, in which she assesses for late Victorian Britain a »supplementation of the elitist ›scientific racism‹ by a popular ›commodity racism‹«, a development that has later been diagnosed for most other Western societies.[10] In close association with the promoted

Anandi Ramamurthy: Imperial Persuaders; Marilyn Kern-Foxworth: Aunt Jemima, Uncle Ben, and Rastus; Deseriee A. Kennedy: Marketing Goods, Marketing Images; and even stronger in broader studies on racism in visual culture or otherness in advertising, as in, amongst others, Anthony J. Cortese: Provocateur; Nana Badenberg: Mohrenwäschen, Völkerschauen.

6 See exemplarily Maurice M. Manring: Slave in a Box; id.: Aunt Jemima Explained.

7 These are widely limited on the U.S. and the figure of the Mammy, as to be seen in Jo-Ann Morgan: Mammy the Huckster; Micki McElya: Clinging to Mammy; Kimberly Wallace-Sanders: Mammy, esp. regarding Aunt Jemima in ch. 3 ›Dishing Up Dixie‹.

8 Jan Nederveen Pieterse: White on Black, esp. ch. 13 ›Blacks in Advertising‹; Raymond Bachollet et al.: Négripub.

9 Cf. Rita Gudermann: Der Sarotti-Mohr; Jean Garrigues: Banania. Find the comment on Garrigues' Banania in Anne Donadey: ›Y'a bon Banania‹, p. 18.

10 Wulf D. Hund: Negative Societalisation, p. 71. Cf. Anne McClintock: Imperial Leather, p. 33 and ch. 5 ›Soft-Soaping Empire‹. See McClintock's concept of commodity racism discussed in various articles in part 2 of Norman K. Denzin's edited book Studies in Symbolic Interaction, especially C.

products and their colonial contexts (like »teas, biscuits, tobaccos, Bovril, tins of cocoa and [...] soaps«), McClintock points out how advertising stimulated the imagination of consumers to »beach themselves on far-flung shores, tramp through jungles, quell uprisings, restore order and write the inevitable legend of commercial progress across the colonial landscape«.[11] The »black person« in her interpretation of this »commodity imagery was not necessarily a reflection of [...] a black person« but rather a »cipher, enabling a white perspective on imperialism to be conveyed«.[12] Thus, to quote Stuart Hall, in the course of imperialism »advertising translated things into a fantasy visual display consisting of signs and symbols« enabling the popularisation of perceptions of superiority that were initially developed in elite discourses.[13]

Applying this methodological approach to abolitionist discourses in the United States, the three images on the cover of this volume reveal a story of how representations of slavery could be utilised for merchandising purposes long after its abolition.[14] In accordance with the text of Harriet Beecher Stowe's *Uncle Tom's Cabin*, both Hammatt Billings, illustrator of the original publication from 1851, and George Cruishank, who drew 27 sketches for the first European edition of 1852, depicted the institution of slavery as violent and immoral. Billings' portrayal of the slave market not only hints at the pyramid-shape of the slave society, with exploited blacks on the bottom and the exploitative slave trader at the top, but also contains a moralisation of this hierarchy, with the whites looking grim and threatening and the black slaves appearing helpless at their mercy.

For the title character of Uncle Tom, salvation comes in the form of a young white girl named Eva, who introduces him to the

Richard King: Commodity Racism Now; and id.: Unsettling Commodity Racism.

11 Anne McClintock: Imperial Leather, p. 219.

12 Celia Lury: Consumer Culture, p.113.

13 Stuart Hall: Representation, p. 333. The connection between Hall's and McClintock's works is mentioned in Debra Merskin: The Princess and the SUV, p. 138.

14 Hammatt Billings' slave market from the first edition of *Uncle Tom's Cabin* is reprinted in Elizabeth Ammons (ed.): Harriet Beecher Stowe's Uncle Tom's Cabin; George Cruishank's ›Tom and Eva in the Arbour‹ was published in the first European edition of *Uncle Tom's Cabin*, London: Cassell 1852; the Cream of Wheat advertisement from 1921 is reprinted in Kenneth W. Goings: Mammy and Uncle Mose.

Bible and teaches him how to read it. As Cruishank's illustration shows, Eva is in possession of the knowledge to guide Tom to a brighter future and Tom faithfully follows his spiritual mentor. While Eva's (or rather Stowe's) Christianity favoured the emancipation of slaves, it did not provide blacks with equality. Following the path that he was shown, Tom ends up appearing in a humiliating advertisement for Cream of Wheat, with Eva's successor still keeping a tight rein on him and with a whip as a clear reminiscence of the violent era of slavery.

Historically, corresponding to patterns of such stereotyping and othering, racism and racial images developed across various discourses and resulted in simplified images applicable for commercial promotion.[15] In the first half of the 20th Century, some of these images were distinctive enough to become the established trademark figures of prominent campaigns in various countries. Using the examples of Uncle Ben in the U.S., the Sarotti-Mohr in Germany and Banania's Tirailleur Sénégalais in France (see figs. 1-3), I will show how a visual language of superiority emerged alongside slavery, Orientalism and colonialism that led to uni-

15 As introductory readings for these concepts see, amongst others, Michael Pickering: Stereotyping; Stuart Hall: The Spectacle of the ›Other‹; Peter Burke: Eyewitnessing, esp. ch. 7 ›Stereotypes of Others‹.

versal but distinct practices of commodity racism.[16] Against the shared background of racial sciences, each country experienced a specific history of racial representation, which is mirrored in racialised advertising that continues to the present day.

Exploring this with comparative studies of the initial trademark stereotypes by reference to their racial features (ch. 2.1), the societal status of their models (ch. 2.2) and the promoted products (ch. 2.3), I will reveal what subtexts each campaign transmitted (ch. 3.1) to reach an exposed position in the respective country's consumer culture (ch. 3.2) and how the critique by social movements resulted in transformations of the figures and attempts toward tolerance and (racial) democracy (ch. 3.3). Against some scholarly objections that »there is no possible innocent reference to a stereotype, and there is no stereotype to denounce until it is quoted«, I will literally and visually refer to stereotypical images, but I hope to do so with sufficient critical and historical embedding.[17]

Fig. 1-3: The trademark figures of Uncle Ben's (1947), Sarotti (1928) and Banania (1915).

16 Fig. 1-3 are reprinted in Michael S. Barnes: The Tom-Caricature; Rita Gudermann: Der Sarotti-Mohr; and Brett A. Berliner: Ambivalent Desire.

17 Mireille Rosello: Declining the Stereotype, p. 38. See also Anne Donadey: ›Y'a bon Banania‹.

2. Histories of Racial Stereotypes

In his analysis of the racial Other, Stuart Hall argues that in the course of modernity alleged cultural and physical features of Africans and their descendants were simplified to a degree that eventually resulted in »black types« reproducible »with a few, simple, essentialized strokes of the pen«.[18] In examining three examples of these types in the figures of the Sarotti-Mohr, Uncle Ben and the Banania soldier, the first step has to be a close look at the meanings and connotations conveyed by them. Thus, the trademark images have to be kept in mind while searching for their iconographic antecedents. First, however, some consideration should be given to the concept of stereotyping and how it informs this research.

As Michael Pickering observes, stereotyping can be understood as a »collective process of judgement which feeds upon and reinforces powerful social myths« and which aims at »warding off any threat of disruption to ›us‹ as the ›same together‹ through the generation of an essentialised Otherness«. Therefore, by linking the traditional idea of stereotypes to the more fashionable concept of othering, Pickering also supports a historical approach to the strategies of social exclusion, »for although theorisations of the Other are relatively recent, representations of the Other go back much further«.[19] Methodologically, this leads to a duality of imagined exclusion. Firstly, an out-group (and therewith logically the in-group) is constituted on the grounds of its supposed otherness. In the second step, though historically in most cases simultaneously, individual Others are stereotyped with regard to various myths and anxieties held by the stereotyping in-group.

In the case of racial stereotypes and, consequently, for the present study, skin colour emerges, not as the only, but as the *prevalent* othering indicator.[20] Following the definition of whiteness, this co-

18 Stuart Hall: The Spectacle of the ›Other‹, pp. 247, 249.

19 Michael Pickering: Stereotyping, pp. 48, 49.

20 See further patterns of historical racisms based on purity, civilisation or chosenness discussed in Wulf D. Hund: Rassismus, pp. 36-81. For the skin colour of white as a social construct that was applicable not just to exclude Africans, but at times also Irish, Jews and underclasses, and historically could include Chinese or Indians see W.E.B. Du Bois: The Souls of White Folk; Alden T. Vaughan: From White Man to Redskin; Walter Demel: Wie die Chinesen gelb wurden; Matt Wray: Not Quite White; Noel Ignatiev: How the Irish Became White.

lour became the »somatic norm« that excluded the »subpersons on the other side of the color line« and ensured the included of »aesthetically and morally, intellectually and culturally« superiority.[21] Within this abstract framework of racial othering, one can now perceive a set of specific, valuing stereotypes for which »›black‹ acts as a packaging term, as for instance in relation to sport and music (where it is given positive value) or crime and violence (where the image is wholly negative)«.[22] With respect to the traditional definition put forth by Gordon Allport, according to which a »stereotype is an exaggerated belief associated with a category«, Kate Lowe similarly finds »positive stereotypes« linked to blackness, which still »have negative implications«.[23] This possible ambiguity of (racial) stereotyping is of particular interest for the following examination, since we will deal with images that were consciously selected (and are retained) because they arouse positive emotional reactions among wide sections of Western populations.

Given this as a methodological orientation, I want to identify in this chapter the historical stages of othering and stereotyping for each of the three figures, concluding with some thoughts on the linkage of the types to the promoted products. In doing this, I will often focus on the perspective of the ›white‹ stereotyping society and, when necessary, contrast it with social realities, but at no time will I make a judgement about existing personalities of stereotyped Others. As George M. Fredrickson puts it, »stereotypes« as »important historical phenomena« tell us »a great deal about those who hold them« and, as I would like to add, very little about their actual objects.[24]

2.1 Others

Looking at our three advertising figures, the most noticeable characteristic they have in common is the colour of their skin. With respect to these images but, for now, regardless of individual shades or physiognomy, the meaning of blackness as a method

21 Charles W. Mills: The Racial Contract, pp. 61, 59; Wulf D. Hund: Die weiße Norm, p. 197. Find a profound analysis of the emergence of the notion of whiteness in Gary Taylor: Buying Whiteness.

22 Michael Pickering: Racial Stereotypes, p. 92.

23 Kate J. P. Lowe: The stereotyping of black Africans in Renaissance Europe, p. 17. She refers to Gordon W. Allport, The Nature of Prejudice, p. 191.

24 George M. Fredrickson: The Arrogance of Race, p. 207.

of othering, wherever possible, has to be examined separately for France, Germany and the United States. Following Peter Burke in his assumption that images constitute an »important contribution to the history of mentalities«, I will focus on visual culture in revealing common roots and differing elaborations of the national discourses on the black Other.[25]

Representations of blackness in European culture can be traced back to antiquity, but at a time lacking »institutional barriers or social pressures against black-white unions« skin colour merely »functioned as a variety of perceptions«.[26] However, with the crusades and legends of Prester John and his Oriental Christianity, the Middle-Ages supplanted ancient colour blindness in a veritable »reappraisal of Africa« leaving a »salient trail in European iconography from the twelfth century onward«.[27] Following the examples of the three Magi who, in their artistic representation, positively portrayed Oriental characters since the 8th century, blacks became a frequent motif in religious paintings: on the one hand symbolising the role of »Africa as the continent just beginning to participate in world affairs«, on the other hand, evoking the myth of global Christianity opposing (and belittling) the Islamic threat.[28] While the black Magus initially represented merely a »signal marker of otherness«; he, in the course of increasing European exchanges with Africa, »absorbed [...] images of the black and blackness« and consequently became the first black »stereotypical character« to function as an artistic device in numerous paintings around 1500 (figs. 4-5).[29]

25 Peter Burke: Eyewitnessing, p. 9. See further evaluations of images as historical sources in Robert I. Rotberg and Theodore K. Rabb: Art and History; and Ivan Gaskell: History of Images.

26 Frank M. Snowden, Jr.: Before Color Prejudice, p. 97; Wulf D. Hund: Rassismus, p. 72. See also Benjamin Isaac: The Invention of Racism in Classical Antiquity, esp. pp. 324-370; and David M. Goldenberg: The Curse of Ham.

27 Jan Nederveen Pieterse: White on Black, pp. 24-28. A further discussion of Prester John and his pictorial displays in Medieval Europe can be seen in Thomas Hahn, The Difference the Middle Ages Makes, p. 11.

28 Joseph L. Koerner: The Epiphany of the Black Magus circa 1500, pp. 10-11; Allison Blakely: Blacks in the Dutch World, pp. 83-86. See further discussions and plentiful illustrations of the Magi in Richard C. Trexler: The Journey of the Magi.

29 Joseph L. Koerner: The Epiphany of the Black Magus circa 1500, pp. 13, 33. Fig. 4: detail from Hieronymus Bosch: Adoration of the Magi (c. 1495).

Figs. 4-5: The black Magus as a frequent feature of Renaissance painting signalised Otherness and faithfulness and, as the first visual black stereotype, still lacked derogatory connotations.

When the first blacks arrived on the American continent, »no one had in mind to establish the institution of Negro slavery« and, on the contrary, accompanying the Spanish and Portuguese conquerors, »[t]hese first Africans to come to the New World [...] were already Hispanicized« and some of them »as freemen [...] became an important component of coastal towns«.[30] Despite this, in North America, English settlers imported a tradition of linking slavery to darkness of skin, as associated in their homeland with Welsh or Celtic bondsmen, and a collection of superstitious beliefs attributed to the colour of black.[31] Moreover, following the »evolution of

This is reprinted in Allison Blakely: Blacks in the Dutch World, p. 90. Fig. 5: detail from Hans Memling: Adoration of the Magi (c. 1470). Reprints can be found in Joseph L. Koerner: The Epiphany of the Black Magus circa 1500, p. 36; Barbara G. Lane: Hans Memling, S.26.

30 Winthrop D. Jordan: White Over Black, p. 44; Audrey Smedley: Race in North America, pp. 141-142.

31 Nell I. Painter: The History of the White People, pp. 34-35. Winthrop Jordan cites the Oxford English Dictionary listing the meanings of ›black‹ »before the sixteenth century«, including »[d]eeply stained with dirt; soiled, dirty, foul. [...] Having dark or deadly purposes, malignant; pertaining to or involving death, deadly; baneful, disastrous, sinister. [...] Foul, iniquitous, atrocious, horrible, wicked. [...] Indicating disgrace, censure, liability to punishment, etc.«, in White Over Black, p. 7.

the concept of unfreedom«, as Youval Rotman calls early clerical condemnations of enslaving Christians in the Byzantine Empire that expanded to Western Europe in the late Middle Ages, the hitherto undisputed institution of slavery had become a moral issue.[32] Initially, this was reflected in the treatment of the American Indians. Although considered heathens and enslaved at the outset of colonisation, their physical exploitation was soon contested, although not entirely eradicated, on ethical grounds, with clerics like Bartholomé de las Casas prominently advocating the replacement »of Indian workers with black African slaves« (figs. 6-7).[33]

Somewhat systematised, but prior to a scientification of race and slavery, the connection of colour and status was strongly based on the belief that the complexion of Africans resulted from a biblical curse that was put on Canaan and his descendants by pro-

32 Youval Rotman: Byzantine Slavery and the Mediterranean World, pp. 131-176.

33 Daniel Castro: Another Face of Empire, p. 74. On explanations for the failure of Indian Slavery in North America see Dorothy Schneider and Carl J. Schneider: Slavery in America, pp. 217-222. Figs. 6 and 7 are newspaper announcements from 1769, reprinted in Barbara E. Lacey: Visual Images of Blacks in Early American Imprints, here pp. 140-141.

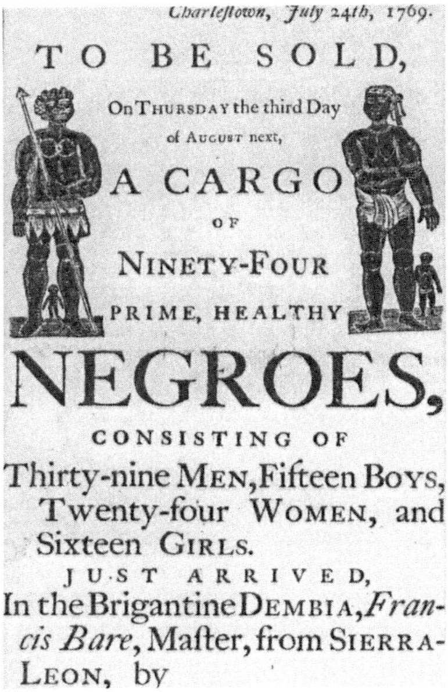

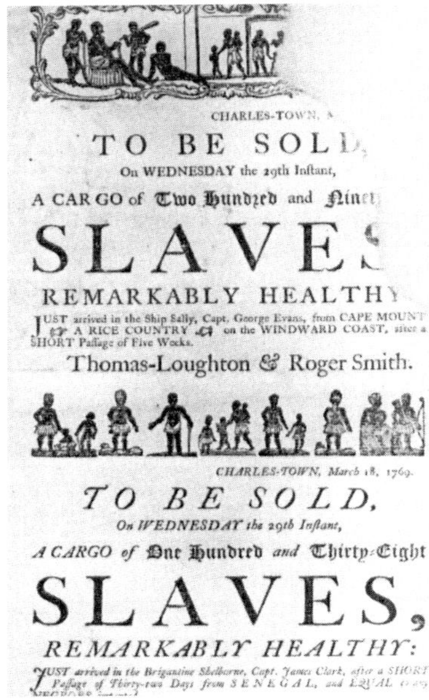

Figs. 6-7: By the early 18th century, ›negro‹ and ›slave‹ had become synonymous in the United States and Africans were perceived as doomed to eternal bondage either because of a biblical curse or due to their natural inferiority.

genitor Noah.[34] Explicitly discussed in Auguste Calmet's *Dictionary of the Holy Bible* of 1732, the link between Ham's offspring supposedly being »burnt, swarthy or black« and eternal serfdom ordained by God became fundamental, especially for U.S. pro-slavery argumentation until the age of abolitionism.[35] With the labour-intensive plantation economy becoming the foundation of most American societies and facing the increasing »›non-enslaveability‹ of Christian whites«, established prejudices, biblical myths and ancient Aristotelian justifications of slavery coalesced to a perception of Africans as »natural slaves«.[36]

34 See different readings of the ›Curse of Ham‹ discussed in John S. Bergsma and Scott W. Hahn: Noah's Nakedness and the Curse on Canaan (Genesis 9:20-27).

35 Stephen R. Haynes: Noah's Curse, p. 38. As an early form of »scientific« racism, Haynes mentions the concept of »Pre-Adamism« or »polygenesis«, this allows the interpretation of »Black Races« or »nonwhite Mongols« as independent from the actual genesis and thus unrelated to the white Christian part of humanity, p. 15.

36 David Eltis: The Rise of African Slavery in the Americas, pp. 57-84. David

Simultaneously, back on the European continent, a new set of images developed in Mediterranean countries, following the »consequent change from the widespread use of white slaves to the widespread use of black slaves within Europe«. Coming as »non-European ›others‹« and forming an obvious »opposition to the characteristics of white, European appearance«, sub-Saharan Africans were labelled in multiple ways, but were almost uniformly perceived as slaves.[37] The close association of blackness with servitude inspired a new genre of paintings, commonly featuring black servants and their white mistresses.[38] Being read as a stylistic instrument which »highlights the whiteness of the skin of the portrait's central subject« or as a »degenerate version [...] of the black Magus attending Madonna«, these black servants mark the birth of the »docile Negro which was taking hold of the West and would live on for centuries« (figs. 8-10).[39]

Unlike early American perceptions, European images of slaves were to a considerable degree influenced by notions of luxury and beauty, culminating in an obsession with the Harem and its sexual connotations.[40] Discovering the existence of black Africans in the course of ongoing confrontations with the Islamic empires, foreign

B. Davis: Inhuman Bondage, pp. 78, 48-76. Nevertheless, up until the 17th century, white indentured servants and convicted criminals worked in British North America and the Caribbean, cf. Don Jordan and Michael Walsh: White Cargo.

37 Kate J. P. Lowe: The stereotyping of black Africans in Renaissance Europe, pp. 17, 20-21.

38 Most scholars interpret Titian's portrait of *Laura dei Dianti* (c. 1523-25) as the prototype of these images. Cf. Paul H. D. Kaplan, Titian's Laura Dianti and the Origins of the Motif of the Black Page in Portraiture; Gary Taylor: Buying Whiteness, p. 41. However, historical controversies on the social status of the portrayed woman challenge the alleged exemplariness of this painting. See Jane F. Bestor, Titian's portrait of Laura Eustochia. For possible Medieval precursors of black servant representations see Dorothy H. Verkerk, Black Servant, Black Demon.

39 Susan D. Amussen: Caribbean Exchanges, p. 192; David Dabydeen: Hogarth's Blacks, p. 36; Allison Blakely: Blacks in the Dutch World, p. 113. Fig. 8: detail from Titian: Laura dei Dianti (c. 1523-5); fig. 9: Peter Lely: Elizabeth Murray, Countess of Dysart, with Black Servant (c. 1650); fig. 10: Anonymous, Die Bedienung (1795). Reprints can be found in Gary Taylor: Buying Whiteness; Susan D. Amussen: Caribbean Exchanges; and in Jan Nederveen Pieterse: White on Black.

40 Nell I. Painter: The History of the White People, pp. 43-58.

peoples became an essential element of the oriental narratives.[41] Thus, Africans that were later enslaved, and especially those held as domestic servants, fulfilled a more decorative function: a practice that interacted with arts in which the »black servant [... was] essentially the eunuch, the emasculated harem servant«.[42] This leads to the conclusion, as Felicity Nussbaum analyses, that »it is clearly counterproductive to reduce Others to Oriental and African«; with respect to the European perceptions of otherness we have to understand the interaction between both concepts.[43]

Long before Mohammed and the spread of monotheism, »the East [...] always held a certain fascination for westerners« constituting the »European view of the ›other‹, like the European view of the ›self‹«.[44] In this context, but bearing modern Orientalism in mind, Edward Said describes the Orient as »essentially an idea, or a creation, with no corresponding reality«.[45] As a negative juxtaposition to Europe, it was charged with all sorts of connotations ranging from obvious accusations of heresy and even Satanism to an implicit recognition for scientific advances and a fascination for alleged sexual openness.[46] Prior to the 17th century, images of this Other within the European borders and anxieties about invasion (for example »Türkengefahr«) dominated the discourses, until the »Muslim states ceased to be a threat politically« and »derisive attitudes [arose] not from an inferiority complex but from a

41 On the early contact of Europeans and Africans in the crusades and before, see Peter Martin: Schwarze Teufel, Edle Mohren, pp. 15-18. The nexus of Christianity and Islam in context of slavery and mastery is described by David B. Davis: »For well over a millennium, the ultimate division between ›Us‹ and ›Them‹, or ›the Other‹, a paradigm for the polarity between masters and slaves, was nourished by the Muslim invasion of eastern and western Europe; by the Christian crusades into Muslim territories; by the Christian reconquest of Portugal, Spain, and the Mediterranean islands; and by the Muslim enslavement, from the 1500s to the early 1800s of well over a million western Europeans from Italy, France, Spain, Portugal, Holland, and Britain.«, Inhuman Bondage, p. 78.

42 Jan Nederveen Pieterse: White on Black, p. 128.

43 Felicity A. Nussbaum: Between ›Oriental‹ and ›Black So Called‹, p. 142.

44 David R. Blanks and Michael Frassetto: Western Views of Islam in Medieval and Early Modern Europe, p. 1.

45 Edward Said: Orientalism, p. 5.

46 Hichem Djaït: Europe and Islam, pp. 9-20. A historiography of these early perceptions can be seen in David R. Blanks: Western Views of Islam in the Premodern Period.

Figs. 8-10: The black attendant accompanying and serving his white mistress is one of the most persistent black images in European iconography. In various countries the attendant was meant to highlight the noble whiteness of upper-class women, frequently in Oriental dress, and to emphasise his role as a symbol of exoticism and luxury.

Eurocentric sense of cultural superiority«.[47] There can be no doubt that orientally dressed black slaves played a part in the symbolic display and the reinforcement about eventual European hegemony, but how then do Africans fit in the binary system of othering between Muslims and Christians?[48]

This vagueness starts with geographical definitions in German scholarship, in which according to Said's classic there never was a »partnership [...] between Orientalists and a protracted, sustained national interest in the Orient«, not knowing where to locate the so-called ›Morgenland‹ and who to perceive as its inhabitants.[49] According to Andrea Polaschegg, the German term ›Mohr‹ from early modern times to the 19th century was not only used to »label the population of the entire African continent, but also served as a synonym for ›Muhammadans‹«.[50] Initially, the ›Mohr‹ in the German imagination was attributed with positive features, was used in emblems of noble families and, in the figure of Saint Maurice, symbolised masculine strength and faith in context of the Wendish Crusade (fig. 11).[51] This perception needed the development of transatlantic slavery and the accompanying devaluations of Africans, to enable the virtual amalgamation of Muslim and colour stereotypes, although, as I will show later, the Sarotti-Mohr proves that older perceptions of the ›Mohr‹ never entirely disappeared.

Ideologically, this geographical and semantic embrace inspired

47 David R. Blanks and Michael Frassetto: Western Views of Islam in Medieval and Early Modern Europe, p. 14. For the notion of »Türkengefahr«, cf. Almut Höfert: Den Feind beschreiben, esp. pp. 51-88.

48 This question does not aim at the physical level of a connection between Europeans, Muslims and Africans. As briefly mentioned above, Europeans observed black African slaves among Muslims since the first contacts. Cf. Ronald Segal: Islam's Black Slaves; Bernard Lewis: Race and Slavery in the Middle East; John Hunwick and Eve T. Powell: The African Diaspora in the Mediterranean Lands of Islam.

49 Andrea Polaschegg: Der andere Orientalismus, pp. 63-85; Edward Said: Orientalism, p. 19. Said's interpretation of German Orientalism has been challenged with respect to Antisemitism and the »politics of theological discourse within the German academy«, in Jonathan M. Hess: Germans, Jews and the Claim of Modernity, pp. 88-89.

50 »Denn mit ›Mohren‹ konnten [...] nicht allein die Bewohner des gesamten afrikanischen Kontinents bezeichnet werden, sondern der Begriff war auch als Synonym zu ›Muhammedaner‹ im Gebrauch.« Andrea Polaschegg: Der andere Orientalismus, p. 75.

51 Gude Suckale-Redlefsen: Mauritius. An image of the statue can be found in Jan Nederveen Pieterse: White on Black, p. 26.

Fig. 11: Erected in 1245 as a symbol for the Crusades against the Slavs, the statue of St. Maurice in Magdeburg shows the black Saint as a brave and pious soldier and exemplifies the positive attributes of the traditional moor stereotype.

beliefs that the »alleged sexual excesses of Muslims or Turks were linked to those of the Moors or Black Africans«, which exemplarily illustrates how two out-groups could be associated by means of one particular pattern of exclusion; in this case the ever-present suspicion of promiscuity contrasted with European morals of abstinence.[52] Additionally, as Muslim armies included African soldiers, the atrocities of war were, in the European imagination, not just linked to the impiety of their enemies, but also to their colour.[53] The zeitgeist of othering had a clear tendency: in attempts to divide ›Oriental blacks‹ from the enslaved ›negroes‹ in the Americas, 18th century travellers like Edward Ives or Jemima Kindersley revealed early propagation of colour hierarchies applicable to different world regions, ranking, for example, »light-skinned men in Allahabad« above »darker Indians elsewhere« on the subcontinent.[54] However negative the Europeans regarded Islam and the Orient, by the end of the 17th century the shade of complexion,

52 Daniel J. Vitkus: Early Modern Orientalism, p. 224.

53 Wulf D. Hund: Rassismus (1999), p. 28. Hund in the following explains how the abovementioned image of the black saint emerges as an antithesis to the black Muslim soldier, pp. 29-31. For further reading see Daniel Pipes: Slave Soldiers and Islam; and id.: Black Soldiers in Early Muslim Armies.

54 Felicity A. Nussbaum: Between ›Oriental‹ and ›Black So Called‹, p. 144.

though not yet scientifically defined, had become an indicator for human qualities and was outshining older patterns of exclusion.

To a considerable extent, and next to his Orientalist symbolic implications (which will be discussed later), the black servant of European iconography still functioned as a reminder of the significant influence of the transatlantic slave trade on economies and societies in the Old World.[55] In his »sartorial elegance« belying the excluding character of blackness and the »sordid reality [...] of naked and manacled blacks in the colonies«, his omnipresence, conversely, symbolised an awareness of the linkage between wealth and Africans; underlined by numerous examples of slaves with their European masters depicted in maritime surroundings, highlighting their distant background and hinting at colonial slavery (figs. 12-13).[56]

The ambivalence of the European perspective on Africans becomes more obvious when considering another branch of images, which show them either in their alleged natural environment or as slaves overseas. Here, the »unease [...] that some whites felt about treating people as things« was appeased by drawing the black as a »violent, treacherous and dangerous being«.[57] Supposedly informed by increasing expeditions to Africa, depictions of black savages portrayed in a surrounding of natural abundance and a state of nature lacking rudiments of civilisation (i.e. clothes) and pious European morality exemplified the cultural gap between ›them‹ and ›us‹.[58] Thus, Africans were considered to live inspired by the wilderness – in conditions of ruthless brutality, with European enslavement as a last resort.[59] A »fear of slave uprising«

55 For the sake of completeness, I should point at the debate following Eric E. Williams' classic approach to the nexus of capitalism and slavery. Cf. Eric Williams: Capitalism & Slavery; Barbara L. Solow and Stanley L. Engerman: British Capitalism and Caribbean Slavery; Heather Cateau, Selwyn H. H. Carrington: Capitalism and Slavery Fifty Years Later.

56 David Dabydeen: Hogarth's Blacks, p. 114; Susan D. Amussen: Caribbean Exchanges, p. 193. Sometimes, as Amussen notices, the oriental trappings were even contrasted with a collar, marking the »status as a slave«. Fig. 12: Gerard Soest: Cecil Calvert, 2nd Lord Baltimore with His Grandson and Unidentified Servant (c. 1635-50); fig. 13: James Worsdale: Elihu Yale with His Black Servant (c. 1690-1700). Both are reprinted in Susan D. Amussen: Caribbean Exchanges.

57 Madge Dresser: Slavery Obscured, pp. 58-59.

58 Jan Nederveen Pieterse: White on Black, pp. 34-39.

59 Most prominently Edward Long legitimised slavery, among various other

Figs. 12-13: When depicted with their white masters, black servants were commonly shown with a collar marking their status as slaves and with additional features (i.e. maps, ships) hinting at the Triangular Trade and at the colonial property of their merchant owners.

was nourished particularly in port cities involved in the slave trade and was reflected in images of the slave as a menacing superman, barely retainable with chains.[60] Even when the institution of slavery was depicted in its most atrocious violence, it was often the black overseers exercising the cruelest punishments, with the victims enduring them in »unbelievable stoicism« that »expressed an inability to suffer which is inhuman« (figs. 14-15).[61]

This tendency of depicting black slaves as in- or, more precisely, sub-human was accompanied by a scientific discourse on nat-

arguments, through assessing an inherent criminality of the blacks, who as heathens practiced far crueller forms of slavery in their homelands, cf. The History of Jamaica, ch. 3 ›Of the Creole Slaves and African Negroes in Jamaica‹. His arguments are discussed in Marcus Wood: Slavery, Empathy and Pornography, pp. 142-143.

60 David Richardson: Through African Eyes, p. 47.

61 Marcus Wood: Blind Memory, pp. 231-232. Fig. 14: George Cooke: Slave on Deck (1801), reprinted in David Richardson: Through African Eyes, p. 47. Fig. 15: William Blake: The Execution of Breaking on the Rack, illustration from John Stedham's *Narrative of a Five Years' Expedition Against the Revolted Negroes of Suriname* (1798), in Marcus Wood: Blind Memory.

Figs. 14-15: While perceived as docile and cultivable in Europe, black slaves were depicted as ruthless and barbaric when located in Africa, in the colonies or on the slave ship.

ural differences, that implicitly justified the full-scale exploitation of Africans for the white European benefit.[62] Already by the beginning of the 18th century, »[b]oth polygenists and monogenists [...] posited blacks at the extreme lower pole in descriptions and classifications of human varieties« but still included them in a discourse on society; by the end of the century this discourse »collapsed into the discourse on nature« and »[h]umans became classified and visually represented along the same lines as flora, according to similar assumptions about visual features«.[63] In his very brief synopsis of a century's scientific progress, Snait Gissis identifies a crucial point: whereas before scientific racism, discrimination proceeded alongside supposedly escapable categories (i.e. religion, status); it now developed a fundamental quality with escape being beyond all humanly possible.

In his *System of Nature* of 1735, Carl von Linné set the tone

62 Wulf D. Hund: Rassismus (1999), p. 16.

63 Snait B. Gissis: Visualizing ›Race‹ in the Eighteenth Century, p. 42. For a brief overview see also Londa Schiebinger: The Anatomy of Difference.

for following debates. Postulating the existence of 4 differently coloured races, supposedly characterised by specific physical and intellectual features and even by typical clothing, Linné made no secret of his intermingling of cultural and biological observations.[64] Thus, in systematising religious and philosophical concepts of inequality, he inspired generations of scientists who tried to scale the alleged deviations and who frequently located Africans in between apes and mankind, regarding them as a kind of missing link in the order of beings.[65] Being reflected in numerous pseudo-scientific visualisations and popular illustrations of fictional and factual literature, skin colour hierarchies and legends of animalistic Africans left the ivory tower of academia and sowed the seeds for everyday racisms of the next centuries (figs. 16-17).[66]

These discourses were watched with interest in North America, most notably though the work of French naturalist Comte du Buffon, who, with his environmental theories, aroused massive condemnation among the colonial intelligentsia. Against his suspicion of the degenerative conditions in America and the resulting retardation of the Indians, Thomas Jefferson, who saw himself as a »Man of America«, developed his observations of the Native Americans, according to which causes for possible differences be-

64 See for example: »3 Fair, sanguine, brawny. European. Hair yellow, brown flowing; eyes blue; gentle, acute, inventive. Covered with close vestments. Governed by laws. [...] 5 Black, phlegmatic, relaxed. Hair black, frizzled; skin silky; nose flat; lips tumid; crafty, indolent, negligent. Anoints himself with grease. Governed by caprice.« Carl von Linné: The God-given Order of Nature, p. 13. On possible origins of the quartet of colours in ancient humoral pathology, see Wulf D. Hund: Rassismus (1999), p. 35.

65 For 18th century philosophers (like Kant, Locke and Hume) on race, see Wulf D. Hund: Die weiße Norm, pp. 180-190. Further readings can be found in Julie K. Ward and Tommy L. Lott: Philosophers on Race, esp. William Uzgalis: ›An Inconsistency not to be Excused‹ and Robert Bernasconi: Kant as an Unfamiliar Source of Racism, pp. 145-166. In the same volume, there is a study of the nexus between 18th century racial philosophy and the old concept of the ›Great Chain of Beings‹, cf. Francis Moran III: Between Primates and Primitives.

66 Exemplarily, the curious fascination about (sexual) relations between monkeys and inferior races is examined in Mary Bellhouse: Candide Shoots the Monkey Lovers, esp. pp. 771-776. Fig. 16: Petrus Camper: Facial angles (1794), in Wulf D. Hund: Die Körper der Bilder der Rassen. Fig. 17: Oliver Goldsmith: Engraving in *An History of the Earth and Animated Nature* (1795), reprinted in Barbara E. Lacey: Visual Images of Blacks in Early American Imprints, p. 148.

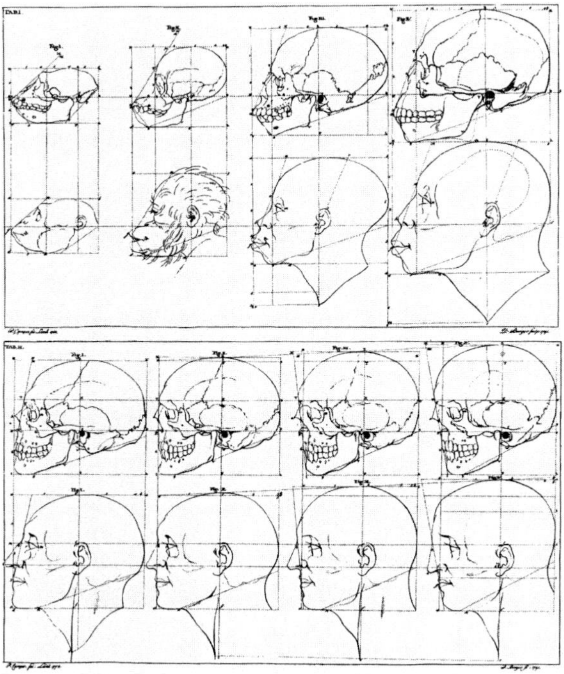

Figs. 16-17: In the late 18th century, ›scientific‹ frameworks of humankind and traditional prejudices coalesced to systematic stereotypes of different races and inspired racial hierarchies, which justified politics of white superiority and located blacks close to apes in biological classifications.

tween Europeans and Indians »are to be found not in a difference of nature, but of circumstance«.[67] On the contrary, with respect to his black slaves, Jefferson willingly speculated about »physical distinctions proving a difference of race« and possible liaisons between orang-utans and black African females.[68] With three classifications of European race taxonomy but a biracial system of slavery to defend, racial science manifested its political impact in the young United States.

As Audrey Smedley puts it in her insightful study on *Race in North America*, the early concepts of racial sciences »reflected popular opinion, and they also portray growing differences in the social roles that different populations in the New World were playing«.[69] Having fought successfully against British oppression and witnessed the unprecedented spread of an ideal of freedom, the American society had to simultaneously integrate a highly diverse (white) population while internalising undisputable justifications for the ongoing disenfranchisement and exploitation of considerable parts of the nation's inhabitants.[70] David Roediger identifies the formation of American working classes in the early 19th century as integral to this process of entrenching racial prejudices, for they defined themselves in political and linguistic dissociation to the institution of slavery and gave birth to the minstrel stages that developed, though initially much more complex, to influence the »defense of slavery« by propagating »the myth of the benevolent plantation«.[71]

Emerging in the urban North and firstly performed solely by white actors in blackface make-up, the minstrel shows became the »first distinctively American and highly successful form of publicly staged commercial entertainment« and eventually the »first

67 Thomas Jefferson: Notes on the State of Virginia, p. 186. Here Jefferson speaks of the »Man of America, both aboriginal and emigrant« and, thus, closely identifies himself with the Indians, cf. p. 192.

68 Thomas Jefferson: Notes on the State of Virginia, p. 265.

69 Audrey Smedley: Race in North America, p. 176.

70 Audrey Smedley: Race in North America, p. 178. See various articles on the influence of the American Revolution on slavery in Ira Berlin and Ronald Hoffman: Slavery and Freedom in the Age of the American Revolution. For a more comparative approach towards the ›Age of Revolutions‹, see David Armitage and Sanjay Subrahmanyam: The Age of Revolutions in Global Context.

71 David R. Roediger: The Wages of Whiteness, pp. 47-54, 66, 115-131; Jan Nederveen Pieterse: White on Black, p. 134.

American musical product exported to the rest of the developed world«.[72] Since the turn of the century, African American characters had been ridiculed in so-called ›Negro songs and dances‹ and were depicted as lacking self-awareness and being vulgar, characterised by overdrawn physiognomies and a notorious pidgin dialect.[73] Inspired by »the minstrel tradition«, contemporary visual arts likewise represented blacks »as largely dehumanized caricatures« in which the »[s]kin color appeared coal black; lips were thick and red, supported by protruding, overly large teeth« (fig. 18).[74] Yet, as Roediger and others have shown, Jim Crow and his blackface fellows primarily served as projection surfaces for »values and actions that aroused both fear and fascination among whites« and could even express the »slashing back at the pretensions and politesse of authority more than at blackness«. [75] However, the »fears of succumbing to a racialized image of Otherness were everywhere operative in minstrelsy« so that all rudiments of identification were ultimately eliminated by a deep awareness of difference.[76]

Although widely considered as pro-slavery folklore and »as a part of the political culture of northern Democrats«, minstrelsy developed racial attitudes »that were often startlingly similar« to the ones of transatlantic abolitionism.[77] For popular culture, Jan Nederveen Pieterse argues, this 19th century phenomenon with its »enormous cultural effect« contributed as strongly to a racist view on society as the institution of slavery itself, which was, howsoever racialised, at the least partly an economic and class problem. The liberation movement developed a notion of »[r]ace [...] as

72 John Springhall: The Genesis of Mass Culture, p. 57.

73 William J. Mahar: Behind the Burnt Cork Mask, p. 329. For origins of blackface masking see Dale Cockrell: Demons of Disorder, esp. pp. 50-54. A discussion of the minstrel dialect can be found in William J. Mahar: Black English in Early Blackface Minstrelsy.

74 A. Everette James: Images of African Americans in Southern Painting, 1840-1940, p. 68. Fig. 18: Show Poster of the Virginia Serenaders (1844), in Stephanie Dunson: Black Misrepresentation in Nineteenth-Century Sheet Music Illustration.

75 David Roediger: Wages of Whiteness, p. 116; W. T. Lhamon cited in Michael D. Harris: Colored Pictures, p. 51.

76 Eric Lott: Love & Theft, p. 25.

77 Mark E. Neely Jr.: The Boundaries of American Political Culture in the Civil War Era, p. 98; Robert Nowatzki: Representing African Americans in Transatlantic Abolitionism and Blackface Minstrelsy, p. 11.

Fig. 18: Beginning in mid-19th century in the United States, blacks were ridiculed in hugely successful minstrel shows with the exaggerated physiognomies of the blackface masks becoming the foundation of popular racist caricatures.

the buffer between abolition and equality«, and in multiple ways »made emancipation conditional – on condition of conversion, on condition of docility and meekness, on condition of being on one's knees«.[78] Coinciding with the formation of a transatlantic popular culture, abolitionism and minstrelsy influenced racial discourses in America as well as in Europe and transmitted narratives of slavery that constituted the breeding ground for most 20th century racial stereotypes.[79]

The blackface mask of the American minstrel show, as the most obvious testimony of veiling the humanity of blacks and as a »cultural overcoding that prevents [...] face-to-face relation« between the races, was brought to Europe by the famous ›Jim Crow‹-inventor T. D. Rice who successfully toured Britain between 1836 and 1843.[80] In a time when the ›negro question‹ was discussed in Eng-

78 Jan Nederveen Pieterse: White on Black, pp. 58-60.

79 See Robert Nowatzki: Representing African Americans in Transatlantic Abolitionism and Blackface Minstrelsy, esp. pp. 166-168.

80 Jon Erickson: The Face and the Possibility of an Ethics of Performance, p. 17; Jacqueline S. Bratton: English Ethiopians, pp. 133-135. For the different tradition of blackface in the English Renaissance drama cf. Robert Hornback: Blackfaced Fools, Black-Headed Birds, Fool Synonyms, and Shakespearean Allusions to Renaissance Blackface Folly.

Fig. 19: In late the 19th century, colonial exhibitions attracted city dwellers in Europe and the U.S., presenting indigenous peoples from all over the world in their ›natural‹ environments and savageness.

lish philosophy and was perceived as one possibility of deflecting social tensions, British minstrelsy lacked American complexity and the »›nigger‹ mask symbolised all that was the opposite of the bourgeois conception of the white English person«.[81] Even if genuine minstrelsy was »inseparable from the social system of slavery« and, consequently, was a racist practice characteristically for the United States, it soon became popular on European stages and inspired a new fashion of racial images.[82]

However, the era of (pseudo-)scientific representations of different races had certainly not ended; though now they tended to follow a more publicly accessible approach. During the recently established world exhibitions in particular, anthropologists tried »to re-create life in the colonies« for the Western civilians to study the »›Other‹ [...] in supposedly authentic houses and shops [...]

81 David T. Goldberg: Liberalism's Limits; Michael Pickering: White Skin, Black Masks, p. 90. See also Alastair Bonnett: How the British Working Class Became White.

82 Katrin Sieg: Ethnic Drag, p. 8. For the influence of American minstrelsy on French representations of blacks see Raymond Bachollet et al.: Négripub, pp. 33-42.

Fig. 20: The World's Columbian Exposition 1893 was accompanied by complex discourses on race, focusing on the relation between supposedly savage blacks from Africa and their ridiculed descendants in the U.S.

follow[ing] a daily routine of artisan work, cooking, eating, and even religious rituals«.[83] Amidst industrial countries competing for the most impressive display of their technological achievements, visitors were ensured of the »savagery and backwardness of Africans«, and ›Völkerschauen‹ guaranteed that this pleasure was not limited to capitals or constricted to temporal intervals (fig. 19).[84] That these images of cultural inferiority did not conflict with the more recent stereotypes of civilised slaves could be observed most strikingly at the 1893 World's Columbian Exposition in Chicago in which Nancy Green, as the first living embodiment of Aunt Jemima, »served, entertained, and sold her products«, and therewith fatally completed the fair's racist spectrum of living exhib-

83 Wolfram Kaiser: The Great Derby Race, p. 52. For some general analysis of representations of white supremacy in context of world fairs see Henrietta Lidchi: The Poetics and the Politics of Exhibiting Other Cultures, esp. pp. 195-198; Loren Kruger: »White Cities,« »Diamond Zulus,« and the »African Contribution to Human Advancement«.

84 Robert W. Rydell: ›Darkest Africa‹, p. 135; Hilke Thode-Arora: Afrika-Völkerschauen in Deutschland. Fig. 19: show poster form 1893, in Anne Dreesbach: Gezähmte Wilde, p. 132.

its, ensuring the »overwhelmingly white visitors« in the so-called »White City« of their superiority over the blackness of either natural savages or domesticated servants (fig. 20).[85] This emergence of marketable Others marks a disruption in the history of racial exclusion and the question of how these convenient stereotypes could develop against the backdrop of the portrayed discourses will be discussed in the following section.

2.2 Stereotypes

During the course of the debate on slave personalities in the American South (initiated by Stanley Elkins' attempt to trace modern stereotypes back to existing role models), scholars like Orlando Patterson and Eugene Genovese identified »Sambo« as »an ideological imperative of all systems of slavery« and as »neither more nor less than the slavish personality«.[86] Similarly, David B. Davis assessed that the »white slaves of antiquity and the Middle Ages were often described in terms that fit the later stereotype of the negro«.[87] However, in reality, »slaves were never ›absolute aliens‹, ›genealogical isolates‹, ›deracinated outsiders‹, or even unreflective ›sambos‹« and even images of them have been more multifarious than the historiography implies.[88] To a large extent, most slave societies have been dominated by a binary imagination of slaves as either dangerous rebels or docile servants.[89] Still, each of the stereotypes was highly complex and could be an amalgamation of several different types, similar just in the degree of submission to slavery. Frequently, the rebelliousness of a slave was linked to his escape from the plantation, as a ›runaway‹ in the U.S. or as a ›maroon‹ elsewhere in the Americas, which leads George Fred-

85 Grace E. Hale: Making Whiteness, p. 151. For the controversies surrounding the 1893 exposition see Elliot M. Rudwick and August Meier: Black Man in the »White City«. Fig. 20: Frederick B. Opper: Darkies' Day at the Fair (1893), reprinted in John Strausbaugh: Black Like You, p. 51.

86 Orlando Patterson: Slavery and Social Death, p. 96; Eugene D. Genovese: Rebelliousness and Docility in the Negro Slave, p. 49. For the debate see Stanley M. Elkins: Slavery, esp. pp. 81-139; Ann J. Lane: The Debate Over Slavery. See a translation, interpretation and history of the slave name »Sambo« in Joseph Boskin: Sambo, pp. 17-41.

87 David B. Davis: The Problem of Slavery in Western Culture, p. 59.

88 Ira Berlin: Many Thousands Gone, p. 2.

89 A concept like this, although with a third type in between the poles, is suggested by John W. Blassingame: The Slave Community, pp. 223-248.

rickson to the assumption that the stereotypes oscillated between the »good Negro‹ in his place and the vicious black out of it«.[90]

Nevertheless, as even Elkins' characterisation of the »Sambo« type conveys, he thinks of the »typical plantation slave« as »chronically given to lying and stealing«, and Patterson likewise provides his »Quashee« with »darker traits« including him being »revengeful, harbouring grudges for a long time [...], ›possessed of passions not only strong but ungovernable [...], indolent, selfish and deceitful‹«.[91] Thus, these figures, whose emergence Patterson located in »the beginning of the second half of the eighteenth century at the latest« really just »designate[d] peculiar Negro character traits« and still rudimentarily contained the stereotype of the docile black servant – bow-tied and grinning – which happened to become one of the most prominent trademark images of the 20th century.[92]

Eugene Genovese interprets the U.S. system of slavery as »determined by particular relationships of class power in racial form« and characterised by a »historically unique kind of paternalis[m]«.[93] Following his approach, this attitude enabled, at least in the master class, a notion of slaves being »childlike and happy, and [...] rel[ying] on the institution of slavery to survive« or, as James Henry Hammond, representative, Governor and Senator from South Carolina, stated, »our slaves are the happiest [...] human beings on whom the sun shines [... but] into their Eden is coming Satan in the guise of an abolitionist«.[94] However, referring to George Fredrickson and his classic study of *The Black Image in the White Mind*, abolitionism and pro-slavery characterisations of black slaves in the U.S. were not necessarily contradictory. In the course of the 19th century, he finds a tendency of conceding positive features to black slaves without questioning their racial

90 George M. Fredrickson: The Arrogance of Race, p. 215. For images of runaway slaves see, Marcus Wood: Blind Memory, ch. 3 ›Rhetoric and Runaway‹. The history of marronage and its influences on slave societies is most profoundly examined in Richard Price: Maroon Societies.

91 Stanley M. Elkins: Slavery, p. 82; Orlando Patterson: The Sociology of Slavery, pp. 175-177.

92 Orlando Patterson: The Sociology of Slavery, p. 174.

93 Eugene D. Genovese: Roll, Jordan, Roll, p. 4.

94 Jennifer Hildebrand: Uncovering the True Relationship between Masters and Slaves, p. 63. Hammond is cited in Kenneth M. Stampp: The Peculiar Institution, p. 430.

difference in an intellectual movement he calls »romantic racialism«.[95] Here, he states, »Northern humanitarians who were more or less antislavery [...] simply endorsed the ›child‹ stereotype [...] of proslavery paternalists [...] and then rejected slavery itself because it took unfair advantage of the Negro's innocence and good nature«.[96]

In her examination of the rape myth in the American South, Diane Sommerville demonstrates how the favourable views on the domestic slaves were especially promoted in post-abolition racism, with its advocates trying to draw a disastrous image of disorder and crime in a post-war multiracial South against »romanticize[d] [...] relations between slave and master«. Noticeably, she emphasises the obsession with black rapists in the late 19th century and contrasts it with testimonies that »denied that slaves of the Old South had posed any sexual threat to white women«.[97] Thus, the docile »Sambo« slave can be interpreted as a stereotype with its roots in paternalistic proslavery agitation, further elaboration and propagation in ›romantic racialised‹ abolitionism and its final destination in postbellum glorifications of the Old South as an antithesis to allegedly criminal blacks after emancipation.[98]

Retrospectively, the slaves were virtually emasculated with reference to the »natural trust and affection subsisting between the two races« and the African Americans lacking any hint of (sexual) criminal energy until »[t]his crime [rape]« developed »when the negro was dominated by the political, religious and social advisors from the North and by the attitude of the Northern press and pulpit«.[99] Feeling generally betrayed by the desertion of their slaves, especially of the »most trusted and pampered slaves – the drivers and [...] house servants«, in the aftermath of the Civil War, this

95 George M. Fredrickson: The Black Image in the White Mind, ch. 4 ›Uncle Tom and the Anglo Saxons‹.

96 George M. Fredrickson: The Black Image in the White Mind, pp. 101-102.

97 Diane M. Sommerville: The Rape Myth in the Old South Reconsidered, p. 486.

98 Find the most prominent example of a racist perspective on the emancipation and blacks turning out of control in Thomas Dixon: The Clansman and its screening in David W. Griffith: The Birth of a Nation. The plot and its impact are analysed in, amongst others, Catherine Silk and John Silk: Racism and Anti-Racism in American Popular Culture, pp. 48-58, 121-133.

99 Henry McHatton and Myrta Lockett cited in Sommerville, ›The Rape Myth‹, p. 486.

»treason« was understood as a result of Yankee influence and constructed in opposition to the Antebellum or even »wartime, when negroes were left on plantations as protectors and guardians of white women and children.«[100] This two-sided perception of the armed black as either protective when kept in certain conditions or as a brutal criminal threatening white women reveals remarkable similarities to later European conceptions of the African as savage warrior or trustworthy colonial conscript.

Despite all racial arrogance, in Europe the notion of a virtuous Other, namely of the noble savage, dates back at least to the first occurrences of racial theories.[101] Initially applied to American Indians only and assuming an innate morality of this »human degree zero«, since the early 19th century Africans were increasingly included in this concept and were seen in context of advancing colonialism: if not as noble, at least as potentially good (i.e. cultivable) savages.[102] Accompanied by ongoing scientific discourse on the question of »whether certain races could spontaneously attain civilization, to what extent, and under what influences«, European missionaries and secular conquerors took on the ›white man's burden‹ and attempted to save African populations from their »beastly and hellish conditions«.[103] ›Freed‹ from their miserable state and forced under white Western rule, the former opponents could even be armed without worries and would support the new mother country in the scramble for Africa.[104] Given that »colonial images are integral to the colonial project« and that the »colonizer can

100 Genovese, *Roll, Jordan, Roll*, pp. 98-99; Myrta Lockett cited in Diane M. Sommerville: The Rape Myth in the Old South Reconsidered, p. 487.

101 Find a comprehensive study of the noble savage in Ter Ellingson: The Myth of the Noble Savage.

102 Jan Nederveen Pieterse: White on Black, pp. 33-39. Nederveen Pieterse differentiates between noble and good savages, implying that while the former is naturally good and in his naturalness less tainted by the evils of modern civilisation, the latter has all the potential of being a civilised man, like a child being stuck in a kind of cultural infancy. Ter Ellingson, on the contrary, sees differences mainly on a semantic level between different languages, assessing that »the English ›noble savage‹ contrasts noticeably with bon sauvage, buen salvaje, and gute Wilde, all sharing attributions of goodness and wildness but lacking the highly charged polarities of the English term«, The Myth of the Noble Savage, p. 7.

103 Cf. Martin S. Staum: Labeling People, esp. ch. 5 ›Ethnology and the Civilizability of Races‹, here p. 157; quotation by missionary Mallet from 1854, cited in Jan Nederveen Pieterse: White on Black, p. 70.

104 Jan Nederveen Pieterse: White on Black, pp. 82-88.

Figs. 21-22: Against persistent stereotypes of barbaric African warriors, blacks could be depicted as loyal soldiers and together with their white commanders when clothed in European uniforms.

gently impose a condition of national selfhood through a massive production of images«, representations of African soldiers, among other colonial motifs, became ubiquitous in the motherlands and were politically charged in the struggle for supremacy (figs. 21-22).[105]

Although colonial troops served in most European armies, it was namely the French government that in the course of the mobilisation for World War I and during wartime itself »praised the commitment and bravery of the black troops«, »[i]nstead of stressing the negative or ›primitive‹ qualities of Africans and African society«.[106] Having had a long history of employing black soldiers, their image in France was moulded in the Revolution and its aftermath, when Toussaint Louverture first led his troops against British invaders in the French colony of St. Domingue but eventually inflicted the most humiliating defeat on the mother country.[107] However, from 1857 onwards the Third Republic offered to Africans »assimilation, that is, the full absorption into the French nation« in exchange for fighting to the death.[108] The con-

105 Anne Donadey: ›Y'a bon Banania‹, p. 10; Tom Conley: Identity, p. 278. Fig. 21: Colonial troops in German South West Africa, in Thomas Morlang: Askari und Fitafita, p. 64. Fig. 22: Lucien Jonas: Journée de l'Armée d'Afrique et des Troupes coloniales (1917), in Raymond Bachollet et al.: Négripub, p. 134.

106 Dana S. Hale: Races on Display, p. 91.

107 Cf. Mary Bellhouse: Candide Shoots the Monkey Lovers, pp. 759-769; C. L. R. James: The Black Jacobins; Pierre Pluchon: Toussaint Louverture.

108 Myron Echenberg: Colonial Conscripts, p. 4.

scious construction of a »force noire« to exemplify the image of a »fraternal partnership [...] with African peoples while maintaining an ideological framework of white racial and cultural superiority« (to which Banania, as to be shown later, substantially contributed) was eventually intended when the Tirailleurs Sénégalais were about to fight on European soil and unleashed a racist outcry in bordering countries.[109] With the black's inherent savagery turned against the supposedly even more barbarous Germans, parts of the French public accepted new representations of the African as vigorous but good-natured.[110]

Described by French authorities as the representatives of »African civilization reborn«, German and British observers did not find much civilised in the colonial soldiers they were seeing on the battlefields.[111] Having developed stereotypes of barbarous African soldiers in earlier wars against the Southwest African Hereros, German intellectuals and media waged a campaign against this »insult, unprecedented, outrageous«, as Thomas Mann perceived it.[112] Backed by international support, most prominently by the British radical E. D. Morel, the racial propaganda intensified in the years of post-war occupation, assuming on the one hand, that France had installed Africans on the enemy's soil »in order to demonstrate [...] the extent of his defeat« and on the other hand, that the colonial soldiers would physically realise the »French defilement of the German Woman« (figs. 23-24).[113] This image of the Tirailleur as potential rapist was not restricted to foreign countries. Citing the cry of »French villagers« who supposedly said that »we

109 Dana S. Hale: Races on Display, p. 92.

110 Nicolas Bancel and Pascal Blanchard, Civiliser, p. 150.

111 Charles Mangin cited in Myron Echenberg: Colonial Conscripts, p. 1.

112 »Man sieht in deutscher Art ein Barbarentum, dessen Kraft gewaltsam und ohne Ansehen der Mittel gebrochen werden muss. Man glaubt, ein Recht zu haben, auf Deutschland Kirgisen, Japaner, Gurka [sic!] und Hottentotten loszulassen – eine Beleidigung, beispiellos, ungeheuerlich, und einzig nur möglich geworden kraft jener im stärksten Sinne des Wortes unerlaubten Unwissenheit über Deutschland.«, Thomas Mann as cited in Christian Koller: Der ›Dunkle Verrat an Europa‹, p. 111. For earlier stereotypes from the Herero wars see Raffael Scheck: Hitler's African Victims, pp. 82-85.

113 Keith L. Nelson: The ›Black Horror on the Rhine‹, p. 606; Iris Wigger: Die »Schwarze Schmach am Rhein«, p. 159 (with the original quote being »Die Schändung der deutschen Frau durch Frankreich«). For E. D. Morel and his part in the campaign against the »Black Shame« see Robert C. Reinders: Racialism on the Left.

Figs. 23-24: Referring to the black troops occupying the Rhineland as hypersexualised savages, German propaganda racially turned the allegedly illegitimate defeat into a »black shame«. Still in 1940, National Socialist media applied the stereotype of the black colonial soldier to justify the war against France.

can no longer let our little girls walk the roads among these savages«, Annabelle Melzer explains the troop movements also as a way to »decrease [... the blacks'] presence in France«.[114]

Meanwhile, in French popular culture a figure had come to existence that was inspired by a notion of »black African soldiers as protectors of France«, but which was represented as a »friendly and harmless character [... with] little in [...] appearance communicat[ing] strength or military preparedness«.[115] As a »grand enfant« the Tirailleur did not just advertise Banania and appear in reports on the black soldiers within the French borders, but this image also served as a rebuttal of the previous »sexualization of the black male« that with the war for the first time became »available to white women« (fig. 25).[116] In the course of its evolution, more-

114 Annabelle Melzer: Spectacles and Sexualitites, pp. 228-229. Fig. 23: Sascha Schneider: Die Schande der Welt (1923), in David Ciarlo: Advertising Empire, p. 318. Fig. 24: Cover of Illustrierter Beobachter (1940), in Julien Fargettas: Les Tirailleurs sénégalais.

115 Dana S. Hale: Races on Display, pp. 94-95.

116 Brett A. Berliner: Ambivalent Desire, esp. ch. 1 ›Tirailleurs Sénégalais and The Making of the Grand Enfant‹, here p. 15. Fig.: 25: French caricature, in

Fig. 25: In French caricature, the African Tirailleur was perceived as friendly but childlike, excluded not only because of his inability to speak adequate French.

over, the stereotype of the childlike, good savage soldier was considerably inspired by American images. In fact, as early as 1870 »most of the black images appearing on posters [in France] had been borrowed from American minstrelsy«.[117] This influence can especially be found in the pictorial connection of »being and [...] physical form«, representing the happy colonial soldier in French iconography with a »flat nose, thick lips, and dark skin – as frames that highlighted the smile«.[118]

With his wide rolling eyes and large red lips, the Sarotti-Mohr likewise reveals a degree of minstrelisation and, indeed, »American minstrel shows toured Europe from the mid-nineteenth century onward and [...] familiarized European and German audiences with the racial stereotypes [... of] the slaveholding and postslavery segregated United States«.[119] As an incarnation of the Oriental moor figure, however, the Sarotti-Mohr evokes images of early modern times and consequently represents aforementioned obsessions about the African as a representative of legendary Eastern

Jan Nederveen Pieterse: White on Black, pp. 84.

117 Leora Auslander and Thomas C. Holt: Sambo in Paris, p. 167.

118 Brett A. Berliner: Ambivalent Desire, p. 23.

119 David Ciarlo: Advertising Empire, p. 219. On the influence of minstrelsy and African American culture on Germany around 1900 see also Astrid Kusser: Cakewalking the Anarchy of Empire around 1900.

luxury and sensuality. From the 13th century onwards, black servants were employed first by German Kings (Hofmohren) and later by princes and merchants to emphasise their wealth, power and the reach of their influence.[120] Surviving multiple changes in racial attitudes, these »noble moors« were still known in late 18th century courts and mansions, frequently dressed in Turkish fashion as an obvious reference to their ostensibly Oriental descent but also to European hegemony, after the Ottoman Wars embracing Eastern customs and traditions.[121]

Although Germany observed discourses on abolitionism and slavery and the development of images of virtuous and noble slaves, and later identified colonial soldiers, if limited to Africa, as »loyal Askari«, the exoticised black servant by the late 19th century still prevailed as a positive stereotype of the racialised Other.[122] Whereas, in reality, most African servants had enjoyed a respectable standing in courts and in society and some even, unlike white working classes, could achieve degrees in higher education such as Anton Wilhelm Amo, who in 1707 initially was »presented as a gift to the Dukes August Wilhelm and Ludwig Rudolf von Wolfenbüttel« and eventually became an »African philosopher of the 18th century«, popular representations frequently portrayed the Hofmohren as children next to their masters and mistresses, with these depictions »aiming not at the actuality of corporeity, but of power« (fig. 26).[123] At the same time, on theatre stages, the black

120 Peter Martin: Schwarze Teufel, Edle Mohren, pp. 41-42. For the special impact of the black chamberlain Johannes Maurus on the early German perception of blacks see Paul Kaplan: Black Africans in Hohenstaufen Iconography.

121 See this exemplarily discussed in the case of Angelo Soliman in Iris Wigger and Katrin Klein: ›Bruder Mohr‹, pp. 83-91.

122 The European debate on slavery as reflected in the German media is portrayed in Barbara Riesche: Schöne Mohrinnen, edle Sklaven, schwarze Rächer, pp. 72-83. Most prominently the image of the noble slave is developed in Johann G. Herder: Briefe zur Beförderung der Humanität, pp. 221-234. Herder's thoughts on blacks and slavery are discussed in Ingeborg H. Solbrig: American Slavery in Eighteenth-Century German Literature. For later imaginations of the »loyal Askari« see Susann Lewerenz: ›Loyal Askari‹ and ›Black Rapist‹.

123 Marilyn Sephocle: Anton Wilhelm Amo, p. 182; »Der Maler hat es offensichtlich nicht auf einen Realismus der Körperlichkeit, sondern auf einen der Macht abgesehen.«, Iris Wigger and Katrin Klein: ›Bruder Mohr‹, p. 92. Fig. 26: detail from Canaletto: Das Gartenpalais Liechtenstein in Wien, reprinted ibid.

Fig. 26: In Europe, black servants were traditionally represented as children, although they frequently enjoyed a good education and social standings in the courts of aristocrats.

attendant took over the part of former white »faithful servants«, with the typical subservience now linked to his colour and his gratitude to the European patron, and authors ranging from Goethe to Hauff fostered the image of the Orient not only as a source of lyrical inspiration, but also as a symbol of otherness.[124]

By the 18th century at the latest, the moor had become an integral part of German everyday culture, lending its name to streets and squares, inspiring emblems of cities and public houses, and making its way into common speech as reflected in sayings and idioms (fig. 27).[125] However, it took the stereotype of the »orientalized Moor« until the 1910s to »come into fashion in commercial imagery«, when, with colonial motifs that were frequently used until World War I becoming more and more obsolete, the »return to exoticism [...] could serve as a distraction from the unrelentingly grim news from the front«.[126] After the war, in the face of attempts to reconstruct German national identity in the abovementioned racial campaign against »primitive black troops« and »question[ing]

124 Barbara Riesche: Schöne Mohrinnen, edle Sklaven, schwarze Rächer, pp. 164-162. German literary imaginations of the Orient are intensively discussed in Andrea Polaschegg: Der andere Orientalismus, esp. pp. 293-448.

125 Cf. Joachim Zeller and Heiko Wegmann: ›Mohren‹. Fig. 27: Coburg coat of arms, reprinted in Peter J. Bräunlein: Von Mohren-Apotheken und Mohrenkopf-Wappen, p. 224.

126 David Ciarlo: Advertising Empire, p. 319. For the representations of colonialism in early 20th century German visual culture see several relevant essays in Volker M. Langbehn: German Colonialism, Visual Culture, and Modern Memory, esp. David Ciarlo: Advertising and the Optics of Colonial Power at the Fin de Siècle; and Joachim Zeller: Harmless Kolonialbiedermeier?.

Fig. 27: The moor as a stereotype in the tradition of late medieval representations of black saints is ubiquitous in German everyday culture and constitutes, for example, the coat of arms of the town Coburg.

France's white ›civilized‹ status«, the German public was not susceptible to imagery that seemed too ethnographic.[127] The fascination with otherness and particularly the Orient, however, was so deep-rooted that the fabulous exoticised African could survive and outlive the »increase in racist violence against black people in Germany« in the 1920s, enabling the Sarotti-Mohr to become »the most visible black figure in German popular culture«.[128]

Decades previously, in American popular culture, the stereotype of the childlike and kind-hearted, but old and simpleminded slave had been consolidated as a racist consensus, reflected in the unprecedented success and countless adaptions of Harriet Beecher Stowe's book *Uncle Tom's Cabin*.[129] Generally, as William Van Deburg states, »novelists of the 1830-60 period [...] abandon[ed] [...] ambiguous portraits of slave characters – choosing instead to create fictional types suitable for use in either the proslavery or antislavery campaigns«, therewith erasing the »adverb ›almost‹ from [...] the black American as ›a Man almost unman'd‹« (figs.

127 Iris Wigger: ›Black Shame‹, p. 35. As David Ciarlo shows, even minstrel shows were perceived as a kind of ethnography by German audiences, Advertising Empire, pp. 219-221.

128 Susann Lewerenz: ›Loyal Askari‹ and ›Black Rapist‹, p. 176; Jan Nederveen Pieterse: White on Black, p. 158.

129 See overviews on the various adaptions and on the impact of the novel on racism and racial stereotypes in Marcus Wood: Blind Memory, ch. 4 ›Beyond the Cover‹; and Patricia A. Turner: Ceramic Uncles & Celluloid Mammies, ch. 4 ›The Troping of Uncle Tom‹.

Figs. 28-29: Through constant reproduction, especially in minstrel shows, Uncle Tom, the main character of Stowe's influential novel, was turned into the ideal personification of the racial consensus in late 19th century America.

28-29).[130] Stowe's main character, although originally introduced by the narrator as a »broad-chested, powerfully-made man«, exemplified this »total absence of [...] ›manhood‹« being caricatured in minstrel shows and folklore, mainly through his natural but unsuspicious feelings towards his master's young daughter, finally claiming in the notorious idiom: »I was born a slave, I have lived a slave, and, bress de lord, I hope to die a slave!«.[131]

As early as 1949, James Baldwin critically noted that »Tom, [... Stowe's] only black man, has been robbed of his humanity and divested of his sex« and through Baldwin's usage of the first name only, he subtly hinted at the importance of the »Uncle« in this process of emasculation.[132] Moreover, as Baldwin states in another essay, the term »Uncle« divides between the two equally demeaning sides of the coin of racial stereotyping: »Uncle Tom, trustworthy and sexless, needed only to drop the title ›Uncle‹ to become vio-

130 William L. Van Deburg: Slavery & Race in American Popular Culture, p. 17. Fig. 28: Hammatt Billings' illustration to the first edition of *Uncle Tom's Cabin* (1852) is reprinted in Elizabeth Ammons (ed.): Harriet Beecher Stowe's Uncle Tom's Cabin. Fig. 29: Poster for *Uncle Tom's Cabin* (around 1890), reprinted in Henry L. Gates (ed.): The Annotated Uncle Tom's Cabin.

131 Harriet B. Stowe: Uncle Tom's Cabin, p. 1; Orlando Patterson defines the »Sambo«-personality as the absence of manhood in Slavery and Social Death, p. 96; Turner cites the minstrelised Tom's lament in Ceramic Uncles & Celluloid Mammies, p. 75.

132 James Baldwin: Everybody's Protest Novel, p. 23.

lent, crafty, and sullen, a menace to any white women who passed by.«[133] In his classic examination of the *Black Family in Slavery and Freedom*, Herbert Gutman comprehends the frequent appellations »Aunt« and »Uncle« as part of slave-naming practices and implies that they derived from the first African groups themselves, who »continued to view kinship as the normal idiom of social relations«.[134] However, used by white masters, »Uncle« soon became a »nonreciprocal term of address that defined an essential status difference between a slave and his or her owners« and carried connotations of unmanliness and serfdom up until the 20th century.[135]

All three stereotypes, which inspired the trademark figures of the campaigns to be analysed, can be interpreted as results of an infantilising »Sambofication« of existing social roles.[136] Each of them represents historical peculiarities of a society and its confrontation with racial Others. Sharing a history of racial theories and having a common notion of racial hierarchies, the United States and France found one way of ideologically integrating inland blacks through their belittlement in popular culture. In Germany, by contrast, Africans were initially not perceived as a domestic issue and, thus, remained a symbol of exoticism and distance, available just to elites and nobility. Referring to an inherent goodness, all of these images were derived from legends of noble savages; particularly in the French and American cases it was the civilising impact of the uniform and servant suit, respectively, that kept the blacks from relapsing into the wild savagery they were saved from. Uniformly presented in minstrel fashion, with the unmistakeable blackness of skin and characteristic physiognomies being evocative of the racial sciences that connected physical appear-

133 James Baldwin: Many Thousands Gone, p. 32.

134 Cf. Herbert G. Gutman: The Black Family in Slavery and Freedom, esp. ch. 5 ›Aunts and Uncles and Swap-Dog Kin‹; Sidney W. Mintz and Richard Price: The Birth of African-American Culture, p. 66.

135 Herbert G. Gutman: The Black Family in Slavery and Freedom, p. 217. How the »Uncle«- or »Uncle Tom«-stereotype was for example considered to exemplify the most contemptible racism in the civil rights movement is examined in Frank A. Petroni: ›Uncle Toms‹, pp. 260-266.

136 Stanley Elkins developed the idea of »Sambofication« with respect to the infantilising effects of slavery on the slave personality. Cf. Benjamin B. Ringer: ›We the People‹ and Others, pp. 170-172. I prefer to follow Jan Nederveen Pieterse who views the process in which »blacks [...] did become childlike dependent creatures« as saying more about the dominant culture than about its racialised objects, White on Black, p. 153.

ance with human qualities, these types, especially in their commodified form, represent the emergence of »racialized objects [... being] simultaneously global and local« in the late 19th century.[137]

In the early 20th century, Germany and France, despite deep preoccupation with racial prejudices, underwent a period of negrophilia (see chapter 3.2), followed shortly by the Harlem Renaissance marking the cultural breakthrough of African American writers and artists in the U.S.[138] Whereas the latter was essentially a movement spearheaded by blacks and symbolised their »project of redefining African Americans« against the stereotypes held by white majorities, the European fashion can be seen as the literal celebration of these images by white city dwellers.[139] Most prominently personified by Josephine Baker, blacks were celebrated on stage and blackness, though condemned in most parts of the public sphere, became a synonym for hilarity and enjoyment in urban night-life.[140] In this atmosphere (which will be part of the examinations in chapter 3), Banania and Sarotti launched advertising campaigns linking their chocolate based products to African characters. How they referred to existing connotations and why Uncle Ben's Rice was deliberately promoted with a docile black slave will be examined in the following chapter.

2.3 Products

As reflected in paintings and language, Susan Terrio asserts that in France »chocolat signified a black man« in the 19th century and »even today it is still a euphemism for people of color«.[141] Similarly, just differently gendered, Kyla Wazana Tompkins interprets »chocolate's color, history, and cultural valences [as to] easily bear the weight of a metaphoric association with the black female body«.[142] Moreover, as Dana Hale observes, blacks used in adver-

137 Leora Auslander and Thomas C. Holt: Sambo in Paris, p. 151.

138 Cf. Petrine Archer Straw: Negrophilia; Astrid Kusser: Cakewalking the Anarchy of Empire around 1900.

139 Anne E. Carroll: Word, Image, and the New Negro, p. 5. For the Harlem Renaissance and racial stereotypes see Andrew B. Leiter: In the Shadow of the Black Beast.

140 Cf. Jan Nederveen Pieterse: White on Black, pp. 138-145.

141 Susan J. Terrio: Crafting the Culture and History of French Chocolate, p. 248.

142 Kyla W. Tompkins: Everything ›Cept Eat Us‹, p. 202.

tising for commodities like coffee and cocoa firstly »represented the color of the beverages« and secondly hinted at the fact that »blacks played an important role in harvesting coffee and cocoa in plantations in America and Africa and [...] had the job of preparing and serving the beverages as servants in European households«.[143] Obviously this connection has multiple implications, but in order to accurately interpret them, the geographical inaccuracies involved it its evolution must firstly be eliminated.

When marketer Dirks Andrees claimed in 1974 that the Sarotti-Mohr was an obvious choice for advertising chocolate since the »moor figure was borrowed from the country of origin of the main raw ingredient, cocoa«, most beans were already imported from West Africa.[144] However, at the time the first black characters were utilised in these promotional activities, »few sensed how important chocolate, and cocoa, would become« for the Gold Coast economies.[145] Having become part of the European experience during the conquest of America, namely in areas stretching from »the Aztec Empire in central Mexico [... to] as least as far south as present-day Nicaragua and Costa Rica«, the consumption of cocoa remained associated with indigenous Americans until the »general demise of small-scale chocolate artisanship« in 19th century Europe.[146] For instance, around the year 1700 colonial produce was clearly arranged in racial terms: »The Chinese man represents tea, the Turk represents coffee, and the Native American represents cocoa«.[147] With its very name deriving from Amerindian vocabularies, French chocolatiers in the 1870s »still had their chocolate ground on metates ›à l'azteque‹«.[148]

Yet, during the same time period, »cocoa companies [...] were [...] develop[ing] an image of an African peasant producer« and just a few years later, »the use of black men, women, and children

143 Dana S. Hale: French Images of Race on Product Trademarks during the Third Republic, p. 138.

144 »Die Mohrenfigur wurde ausgeliehen aus dem Herkunftsland des Hauptrohstoffes, des Kakaos.«, Dirks Andrees: Der Sarotti-Mohr, p. 132.

145 See a history of cocoa planting and economy in Órla Ryan: Chocolate Nations, p. 5.

146 Marcy Norton: Sacred Gifts, Profane Pleasures, pp. 1, 263.

147 Anandi Ramamurthy: Imperial Persuaders, p. 65.

148 Sophie D. Coe and Michael D. Coe, The True History of Chocolate (London, 1996), pp. 117-119, 236. Metates were the traditional curved grinding-stones.

Fig. 30: One of the tasks of the European black servants, which established later racial connotations to cocoa products, was to hand expensive chocolate drinks to the mistress.

to sell chocolate was ubiquitous« in most European societies.[149] One early antecdote the Sarotti-Mohr most directly refers to was that chocolate in Europe was frequently handed to wealthy consumers by black servants, a connection that was reflected in contemporary iconography (fig. 30).[150] In the upper classes, a notion of the »seductive beauty of the exotic« emerged, which constructed a connection between black attendants and the consumption of »hot chocolate«, sometimes from »pots and porcelain demitasses in Oriental style«.[151] On this material level, David Barker notes that in the linkage of chocolate with blackness the »sense of black labour in the production of a luxury item for whites was carried through«.[152]

The »taste for sweetened and spiced chocolate« developed in late 16th century Spain, but was limited for a long time to the upper classes and aristocracy due to the high price of the product. Because of this restrictiveness, the »plantations were to add

149 Anandi Ramamurthy: Imperial Persuaders, p. 63.

150 See for examples of Hogarth's paintings David Dabydeen: Hogarth's Blacks, p. 87; and Sara D. Schotland: Africans as Objects. Fig. 30: Jean-Baptiste A. G. d'Agoty: Madame Du Barry à sa Toilette (c. 1769-86), reprinted in Suzanne Perkins: Is It a Chocolate Pot?.

151 Beth F. Tobin: Picturing Imperial Power, p. 33; Madeleine Dobie: Trading Places, p. 61.

152 David Barker: Identity and Psychopathology, p. 71.

mercantile zest to an Ancien Régime that might otherwise have sunk into lethargy«.[153] Moreover, Werner Sombart interpreted the trade with and the »production of cocoa, coffee, and sugar in the overseas colonies« as »outstanding factors in the development of capitalism«, since they inspired a »love of luxury« that made the economies of »European centers« flourish.[154] Gradually, the »›baroque chocolate‹ [...] spread down the social scale« following a price drop in sugar and the opening of coffee or chocolate houses across Europe with their beverages symbolising exclusiveness and wealth both on the individual and on the collective level in contexts of class and colonialism.[155]

Although there have been boycotts and protests against products associated with slavery since the late 18th century, chocolate remained an integral element of consumer culture and continued to be linked to ›positive‹ black figures.[156] Despite the fact that particularly »French planters specialized [...] in cocoa« and the French Antilles became one of the largest suppliers of raw material for chocolate, France has an almost uninterrupted history of consuming and positively representing this controversial colonial product.[157] After chocolate became more affordable with the addition of milk and the development of the cocoa press in the early 19th century, however, some marketers employed race-neutral images such as scenes from dairy farming for their advertisements.[158] Nevertheless, by the late 19th century the prevailing

153 Robin Blackburn: The Making of New World Slavery, pp. 148, 301.

154 Werner Sombart: Luxury and Capitalism, p. 99; Sidney W. Mintz, Sweetness and Power, p. 139.

155 Robin Blackburn: The Making of New World Slavery, p. 19. Susan J. Terrio: Chocolate.

156 Cf. Charlotte Sussman: Consuming Anxieties; Lawrence B. Glickman: ›Buy for the Sake of the Slave‹.

157 Arthur L. Stinchcombe: Sugar Island Slavery in the Age of Enlightenment, p. 9. With regards to coffee and sugar, the nexus of European consumption, enslavement of Africans and expropriation of Indians was strikingly summarised by J. H. Bernardin in 1773: »I do not know if coffee and sugar are essential to the happiness of Europe, but I know well that these two products have accounted for the unhappiness of two great regions of the world: America has been depopulated so as to have land on which to plant them; Africa has been depopulated so as to have the people to cultivate them.«, cited in Sidney W. Mintz: Sweetness and Power, prefix.

158 Emmanuel O. Afoakwa: Chocolate Science and Technology, p. 2; Virginia Westbrook: Role of Trade Cards in Marketing Chocolate During the Late 19th Century; and Margaret Swisher: Commercial Chocolate Posters.

motif for the promotion of cocoa products was either »just the exoticism of black people and their skin« or »labourers working [on] tropical plantations, producing raw materials for European consumption«.[159]

But cocoa did not just make for an ostensible luxury good and status symbol. As the »first stimulant beverage used in Europe« allegedly inducing a »sexually charged vitality«, it also contributed to stereotypes of the black as sensual and libidinous.[160] As Erica Owens and Bronwyn Beistle convey, the metaphorical transformation of the »black body to an object for consumption« carries sexual meanings that exemplify the racist construction of the black as likewise seductive and pollutant.[161] On the one hand, blackness is associated with all conceivable evils and the »Negro is the symbol of sin«; on the other hand, »blackness evokes an attractive, but dangerous, sexuality, an apparently abundant, limitless, but threatening, fertility«.[162] Whereas the former element is analogous to »the myth of African cannibalism«, the latter to a certain degree inspires fantasies of consuming the Other, by which the »fear of losing whiteness by having a nonwhite child« is potentially »mitigate[d]«.[163] Eating chocolate that is explicitly linked to black bodies, thus, becomes a way of bypassing tabooed miscegenation and satisfies the illegitimate craving for black sexuality.

As early as the late 17th century, French aristocratic mistresses could, with a wink, blame their delivery of a black child on the consumption of »too much chocolate«.[164] Deriving from this connotation, a perception of male black sexuality occurred that was contrary to the obsessions with brutal rapists present at the same

159 Anandi Ramamurthy: Imperial Persuaders, p. 65; and ch. 3 ›Cocoa Advertising, the Ideology of Indirect Rule and the Promotion of the Peasant Producer‹.

160 Marcy Norton: Sacred Gifts, Profane Pleasures, pp. 3, 15.

161 Erica Owens and Bronwyn Beistle: Eating the Black Body, p. 201.

162 Frantz Fanon: Black Skin White Masks, p. 134; Robert J. C. Young: Colonial Desire, p. 97.

163 Joel Kovel: White Racism, p. 66., Erica Owens and Bronwyn Beistle: Eating the Black Body, p. 204. See a discussion of cannibalism and its reversion in the Black Atlantic discourse in Alan Rice: ›Who's Eating Whom‹; and the supplemented chapter of the same name in his book Radical Narratives of the Black Atlantic (London etc., 2003).

164 Bertram M. Gordon: Chocolate in France, p. 573. This incident is also referred to in Isabell Cserno: Pancakes, Chocolate, and the Trap of Eternal Servitude, p. 78.

time. Nederveen Pieterse, for example, identifies an image of »mixed couples [...], in which the black man is almost invariably depicted as grotesque«, being either characterised with »swollen lips« and »sweet as chocolate« or as a »primitive barbarian« and »colossal brute«. The perverted eroticism of the former characterisation ridiculed the black man further by allotting to him a »position socially or physically inferior to that of the [white] woman«, often leaving him as a child or childish figure that could be enjoyed like a piece of chocolate (fig. 31).[165]

Thus, most Western societies, although not always in sexual contexts, developed a tradition of ›edible blacks‹ that associated the consumption of sweets with blackness.[166] Whereas in the U.S. the »notion [was] viciously promulgated by Southerners that black children were only suited for ›gator bait‹« (a stereotype that was frequently exploited for advertising), Europeans metaphorically ate the chocolatey Africans themselves.[167] In Spain, black Conguitos were promoted as naked savages armed with spears, but in the form of cocoa-covered peanuts were lacking any hint of threat or seriousness.[168] Similarly, German-speaking consumers are familiar with chocolate ›Negerküsse‹, ›Mohrenköpfe‹ and ›Eismohren‹, which promise the »eroticized pleasure of reverse cannibalism«.[169]

Being promoted as an amalgamation of the »black strength of cocoa« and the »energy and sunshine of bananas«, the »breakfast cereal made from banana flour, barley, chocolate, and sugar« better known as Banania also linked the various racial connotations of the two main ingredients.[170] While the cultivation of bananas originated in Southeast Asia and spread with the Islamic Empire to Muslim Iberia and throughout wide parts of Africa, the fruit

165 Jan Nederveen Pieterse: White on Black, p. 184. Fig. 31: Chochotte prend son chocolat dans son lit, caricature from *Le Rire* (c. 1900), reprinted ibid.

166 Reference to ›edible blacks‹, or ›essbare Schwarze‹ is made in Jan Nederveen Pieterse: White on Black, p. 159; Stefanie Fock: ›Un individu de raça negroide‹, pp. 171-172.

167 Marilyn Kern-Foxworth: Aunt Jemima, Uncle Ben, and Rastus, p. 31. See also David Pilgrim: The Picaninny Caricature.

168 The transformations of the Conguito figure are briefly considered in Stefanie Fock: ›Un individu de raça negroide‹, p. 171.

169 »[...] als erotisierten Genus seines umgekehrten Kannibalismus«, Stefanie Fock: ›Un individu de raça negroide‹, p. 171. For ›Negerküsse‹ etc. see further Regina Bendix: Of ›Mohrenköpfe‹ and ›Japanesen‹.

170 Susan J. Terrio: Crafting the Culture and History of French Chocolate, p. 250; Brett A. Berliner: Ambivalent Desire, p. 10.

Fig. 31: Especially in French iconography, chocolate became increasingly connoted with black sexuality, frequently equating ridiculed black men with easily consumable sweets.

was not frequently consumed in Europe and North America until the late 19th century.[171] By this time, the international banana trade was largely dominated by U.S. corporations operating in Central and South America. These companies, which developed a modern plantation network, became so powerful that they could impose their will on politics, turning some of the smaller Latin American countries into so-called ›banana republics‹.[172] That this process of capitalist expansion into the developing world proceeded under American military pressure in the ›banana wars‹ is implicitly contained in the uniform and armament of Bonhomme Banania who, thus, represents not only the process of civilising Africa but also the military triumph of Western monopoly capitalism on the banana plantations of the Americas.[173]

In Europe, early images of the banana oscillated between co-

171 Andrew Watson: Agricultural Innovation in the Early Islamic World, p. 54; John C. Robinson and Victor G. Saúco: Bananas and Plantains, pp. 2-3.For further information on the history of bananas see Dan Koeppel: Banana.

172 See for example and with special focus on the United Fruit Company, Alison Acker: Honduras; Peter Chapman: Bananas; Marcelo Bucheli: Bananas and Business.

173 Cf. Lester D. Langley: The Banana Wars.

lonial African and exoticised Latin American connotations.[174] German advertising campaigns were »directly tied to the colonial project« and the motif most frequently used showed »two black figures straining under the load« of banana trees.[175] Amongst others, Sarotti, years before the introduction of their famous icon, referred to the African harvesters in promoting a new banana-cacao powder and integrated the fruit in the national discourse on black savagery and the responsibility of imperialism (fig. 32).[176] The element of savagery, although explicitly eroticised, was later transmitted by singer Josephine Baker, whose banana-skirt symbolised a »girdle of phalluses« marking her as »sexually active, an aggressively promiscuous vamp, a prey turned hunter, sexually available but with the added frisson of the threat of castration«.[177] Nevertheless, the image of the licentious, exotic female popularised in the context of the banana trade cannot be interpreted as a European fantasy of Africa. Since Columbus' expeditions, this stereotype had been linked rather to women of the Caribbean and in the early 20th century, still, it was the picture of a »light-skinned [...] ideal Antillaise« that Banania first used in promotions.[178] Generally, Nederveen Peterse notices, the »Africans or blacks« one can »encounter [...] in French popular culture« are »mainly from the West Indies« and, likewise, the sexualised woman advertising bananas was either a Caribbean or Latin American, but not an African character.[179]

In the Americas themselves, U.S. businessmen exported the racial order of their segregated homeland and soon the cultivation of bananas became embedded in various conflicts alongside colour lines.[180] As Darío Euraque shows for the case of Honduras, it was

174 Although recent forms of racism refer to the banana as a symbol of the alleged monkeyishness of blacks, there is no evidence for this connotation in the early 19th century. Cf. Wale Hudson-Roberts: Levelling the Field.

175 David Ciarlo: Advertising Empire, pp. 300-301, 204.

176 Rita Gudermann: Der Sarotti-Mohr, pp. 64-65. Fig. 32: Advertising poster (1911), in David Ciarlo: Advertising Empire.

177 Jon Kear: Vénus noire, p. 62.

178 Brett A. Berliner: Ambivalent Desire, pp. 10-11. For early sexual connotations of the Caribbean see Wulf D. Hund: Bikini – Die unglücklichen Inseln, pp. 871, 877-878.

179 Jan Nederveen Pieterse: White on Black, p. 161. The racialisation of the Latina in context of banana images is examined in Myra Mendible: Embodying Latinidad, esp. pp. 9-11.

180 Jason M. Colby: ›Banana Growing and Negro Management‹.

Fig. 32: As a classical product of the colonies, bananas were advertised as part of the imperial project and overtly portrayed the exploitation of the African workforce as one main ›ingredient‹ of the fruits.

only the immigrants from the West Indies who worked in the banana economy, that were agitated against and whose »blackness« was perceived as a »threat to the ›mestizo‹ nation« by »Honduran intellectuals and wide sectors of the population«.[181] The negative associations of blackness with immigration and poverty coalesced with the image of the banana and today, in the multiracial United States, blacks from the West Indies are still referred to as »black monkeys coming by the banana boat« by racist African and European Americans.[182] Nevertheless, U.S. intersections of race and consumption go beyond colonial produce or luxury goods and, contrary to the supposedly exotic products that are advertised in Europe with Bonhomme Banania and the Sarotti-Mohr, Uncle

181 Darío A. Euraque: The Threat of Blackness to the Mestizo Nation, here p. 231.

182 Vilna B. Bobb: Neither Ignorance nor Bliss, p. 218.

Ben embodies an everyday commodity which, in a different way, can be associated with the colour of his skin.

To reveal the various connections between rice and blackness in the United States, the historical debate on the influence of African traditions of rice cultivation on the plantation landscape in the Americas must be taken into consideration. Initially »posit[ing] that skilled rice farmers from Upper Guinea introduced technology useful for the establishment and expansion of the eighteenth-century rice-based plantation system« just in »the lowlands of South Carolina and Georgia«, later-historians extended and modified this »black rice thesis« for its application to the slave society in Northern Brazil.[183] As early as 1974, Peter Wood drew scholarly attention to the »fact that the mastery of rice paralleled closely in time with the emergence of a black majority in the colony's population« and in 2003 Judith Carney explained the »choosing [...] of a black farmer to promote the consumer product known as Uncle Ben's Converted Rice« with the close association of »black Americans with rice culture«.[184]

Despite the »black rice thesis« being challenged in a recent publication and although the image of Uncle Ben is neither primarily evocative of a »rice farmer« nor the embodiment of the rice cultivating slaves from West Africa »surviv[ing] in a product carrying the image of one descendant«, the linkage of blacks to this particular crop had certainly influenced American perceptions of rice.[185] After rice initially enjoyed an ambiguous reputation for being nutritious and undemanding, but also for allegedly disseminating malaria, American planters like Thomas Jefferson identified the crops from Africa as »the best rice in the world« and henceforth associated, of all sorts, particularly white rice with African

183 Walter Hawthorne: From Africa to Brazil, pp. 138-139. For classic approaches to the »black rice thesis« see Daniel C. Littlefield: Rice and Slaves; Judith A. Carney: Black Rice. Its application for comparative studies and the case of Brazil can be found in Edda L. Fields-Black: Deep Roots; Judith A. Carney: ›With Grains in Her Hair‹; Walter Hawthorne: From Africa to Brazil, ch. 4 ›Labor over ›Brown‹ Rice‹.

184 Peter H. Wood: Black Majority, p. 36; Judith A. Carney: The African Antecedents of Uncle Ben in U.S. Rice History, p. 1.

185 David Eltis, Philip Morgan and David Richardson: Agency and Diaspora in Atlantic History; Judith A. Carney: The African Antecedents of Uncle Ben in U.S. Rice History, p. 2.

origin and methods of cultivation.[186]

In the late 19th century in France, when »images of blacks« were used to »sell products of either colonial origin or ones closely associated with ostensibly black preferences and tastes«, rice together with »cotton, coffee, cocoa, tropical fruit, [and] rum« were exemplary of the »first instance«.[187] In America, on the contrary, the consumption of rice was strongly attributed to blacks, however the white-dominated marketing industry did not advertise it at all until the 1940s, when Uncle Ben's rice »was the first raw commodity to be given a brand name«.[188] Until the 1950s, rice was eaten in a »striking[ly] [...] regional pattern« and »heavy consumption [...] occurred in areas with a history of rice production and in areas with large numbers of immigrants or their descendants from traditional rice-eating cultures«.[189] Those cultures, however, were not solely African communities, but largely Asian groups dwelling on the Pacific coastline since the early 19th century.

Like bananas in European popular culture are associated with Latin America rather than with Africa, rice unfolds racial connotations that are even stronger in association with Asian Americans than with blacks. In accordance with first doubts about the wholesomeness of rice, Chinese immigrants in 19th century California were accused by Unionists of bringing »nothing but filth, vice and disease«, a conflict that was racially encapsulated with a pamphlet entitled: »Meat vs. Rice: American Manhood vs. Asiatic Coolieism: Which Shall Survive?«.[190] This connection of cheap and unmanly labour with cheap and unmanly food was paralleled with similar discourses on the emancipated blacks, the other ideological opponent of the racist labour movement. Widely perceived as criminal and thievish, free blacks were particularly suspected of stealing their uniformly preferred foods: chicken and watermelons. In 1947, Peter Noble identified the »chicken and water-melon eater« as one of the »principal stereotypes of the Negro in the

186 Letter by Benjamin Vaughan to Thomas Jefferson cited in Judith A. Carney: Black Rice, p. 148. Cf. Peter H. Wood: Black Majority, ch. 2 ›Black Labor – White Rice‹.

187 Leora Auslander and Thomas C. Holt: Sambo in Paris, p. 167.

188 Janice Jorgensen: Encyclopedia of Consumer Brands, p. 608.

189 James R. Shortridge and Barbara G. Shortridge: Patterns of American Rice Consumption, p. 419.

190 Leaders of the American Federation of Labor (AFL) cited in Gwendolyn Mink: Meat vs. Rice (and Pasta), p. 157.

American mind« and Donald Bogle added that »coons emerged as no-account niggers [...] good for nothing more than eating watermelons and stealing chicken«.[191] On the one hand, the traditional »implication [...] that blacks are natively libidinal« was upheld in their chase for the femininely connoted meals of chicken and watermelons (in contrast to masculine food like beef and corn). On the other hand, this perception was one elementary part of virtually emasculating blacks in popular culture (fig. 33).[192]

Aside from the level of consumption, however, blacks in the U.S. were also positively associated with food, either as natural cooks or as servants both in narratives of the good Old South and in the reality of urban gastronomy.[193] Thus, in former rice-States, »black waiters and cooks as loyal servants [...] perpetuated white Creole culinary traditions by preserving old recipes and [...] reinforced black social and economic subservience to white patrons«.[194] Like the mastery of rice cultivation, the knowledge of how to cook, arrange and even to serve the traditional dishes remained associated with blacks. Their own preference for the consumption of rice, however, could still be integrated in discourses on their alleged unmanliness and their racial difference to genuine American qualities.

As all of these connotations and incidents show, European and U.S.-American perceptions of particular foods were shaped under the influence of socio-economic processes and in interaction with common beliefs about race to eventually enable the emergence of complex images of difference, in which commodity and otherness became inextricably linked to each other. Marketers used the resulting images to encourage the public to virtually consume the Other and to shop for a ›different‹ experience, with »race and ethnicity« as a »serious category on which selections were based«.[195] Clearly the specific processes of commodification differed con-

191 Peter Noble: The Negro in Films, pp. 11-12; Donald Bogle: Toms, Coons, Mulattoes, Mammies & Bucks, p. 9.

192 J. Emmett Winn: Documenting Racism in an Agricultural Extension Film, p. 38. Fig. 33: Dish Towel (c. 1940s), in Kyle Husfloen (ed.): Black Americana Price Guide.

193 The obsession with female black cooks in particular is discussed in Alice A. Deck: ›Now Then – Who Said Biscuits?‹.

194 Anthony J. Stanonis: Creating the Big Easy, p. 229.

195 Bell Hooks: Black Looks, p. 23. Hooks generally refers to the commodification of otherness as ›Eating the Other‹, pp. 21-39.

Fig. 33: In the United States, blacks were associated with patterns of consumption which stigmatised them as other, different and feminine, a process that was similarly applied to Asian immigrants.

siderably between the cases of Sarotti, Banania and Uncle Ben regarding, for example, the different connotations each individual trademark figure transmitted and the particular role the commodity fulfilled in its respective country. Nevertheless, resulting from a global discourse of racialisation and becoming part of an international popular and commodity culture, all three products (and their campaigns) can be interpreted according to similar patterns.

3. The Commodification of Racial Images

By the late 19th century, other ethnicities and their cultures became commodified in various ways. Wealthy Europeans started to furnish their houses in colonial style and the growing demand for ›original‹ samples of exotic living resulted in »greatly increased replications of ›traditional‹ objects«.[196] Art and music reflected imperial advances and ethnography moved from museums to fairgrounds eventually arriving in the mainstream and becoming part of popular culture.[197] Soon this colonial trend was accompanied by a European period of ›negrophilia‹ in which »celebrated African American musicians, artists, and novelists [...] found a welcome contrast to American racism in their reception in Paris« and other metropolises in Europe.[198] As not only David Ciarlo and Anandi Ramamurthy have shown, European advertising has to be seen as part of these popular colonial and racial discourses, whereas U.S. American commodity racism mostly referenced Antebellum times and the racial controversies in the aftermath of emancipation. Before going into the individual campaigns, however, some words should be spent on the theoretical implications of advertising and on the question of how otherness was used to affect increasing sales.

The 19th century saw not only the much-cited industrial revolution, but also a consumption revolution that – according to some scholars – only made the former possible in the first place.[199] Simultaneously, printed publications, which according to Benedict Anderson and Francis Bacon »had changed ›the appearance and state of the world‹« as early as 1600, reached more and more sections of the general public.[200] Together with world exhibitions as »places of pilgrimage to the commodity fetish«, print media transmitted not merely a new sense of increasing diversity on

196 Ruth B. Phillips and Christopher B. Steiner: Art, Authenticity, and the Baggage of Cultural Encounter, p. 9.

197 See different elements of this commodification and popularisation of race and ethnicity in the contributions to John M. MacKenzie's edited book on Imperialism and Popular Culture.

198 Leora Auslander and Thomas C. Holt: Sambo in Paris, p. 169.

199 Cf. Daniel Miller: Material Culture and Mass Consumption, esp. pp. 134-138; John R. Hall, Mary J. Neitz and Marshall Battani: Sociology on Culture, esp. pp. 118-139.

200 Anderson quotes Bacon in Imagined Communities, p. 37.

growing markets, but at the same time delivered illustrative material of white superiority to demographic groups hitherto excluded from the benefits of whiteness and consumption.[201] Thus, to quote Burton Benedict, world's fairs »were not only selling goods, they were selling ideas: ideas about relations between nations, the spread of education, the advancement of science, [...] [t]hey were presenting an ordered world«.[202] The connections between the emerging commodity culture, race, and colonialism are observed by Stefanie Wolter, who refers to the abovementioned discourses and the resulting stereotypes (see chapter 2.1 and 2.2) as the creation of ›signs‹ that could now be used for merchandising purposes and »on a symbolical level addressed the ideology of mainstream society«.[203]

As Jackson Lears notes in the introduction to his award-winning study of the history of American advertisements, ads »urge people to buy goods« by simultaneously »focus[ing] private fantasy« and »subvert[ing] existing structures of economic and political power«.[204] This subversion is recognised as imaginary by Judith Williamson, who states that advertisements »obscure the real structure of society by replacing class with the distinctions made by the consumption of particular goods«.[205] Originally only referring to working classes, Willliamson's interpretation can also inform the study of racial stereotypes in advertising when combined with the work of Anja Weiß whose Bourdieuian approach to racism finds that especially »persons with a low level of economic and cultural capital experience racist symbolic capital as a central and explicit dimension of their class position«.[206] Thus, advertising potentially functions to suggest »the consumer's not-belonging to

201 Walter Benjamin: The Arcades Project, p. 7. Carol Breckenridge states that »world fairs [...] created an imagined ecumeme (in much the same way that Benedict Anderson [1983] talks about print media creating imagined communities underlying the nation-state)«, The Aesthetics and Politics of Colonial Collecting, p. 196.

202 Burton Benedict: The Anthropology of World's Fairs, p. 2.

203 »Die Werbung für industriell gefertigte Massenware appelliert somit auf einer symbolischen Ebene an die Ideologie der Mehrheitsgesellschaft.«, Stefanie Wolter: Die Vermarktung des Fremden, p. 46. For the concept of sign, signifier and signified in cultural studies see Tim O'Sullivan et al.: Key Concepts in Communication and Cultural Studies, pp. 284-285, 288.

204 Jackson Lears: Fables of Abundance.

205 Judith Williamson: Decoding Advertisements, p. 13.

206 Anja Weiß: Racist Symbolic Capital, p. 48.

the working class but also confirm[s] him of whiteness« through the usage of racially connoted visual languages.[207]

Wolfgang Fritz Haug describes the »unleashed commodity-cash nexus« as dominated by the »contradiction between buyer and seller, use-value and exchange-value«. On the market, products with similar or equal utility have to create an additional perceived-value in order to produce a »second skin, which as a rule is incomparably more perfect than the first«. This process results in the »aesthetic abstraction of the commodity [that] detaches both sensuality and meaning from the object as a carrier of exchange-value and makes the two separately available«.[208] Competing, thus, in terms of the meaning or the promised-value rather than of the real use-value, the existential importance of advertising and image becomes obvious. For this purpose, some marketers still perceive stereotypes as the »best way to [...] get directly to a storyline that will sell«.[209] As this analysis will demonstrate against the backdrop of nation-specific racial discourses, in the cases of Uncle Ben, Sarotti and Banania the stereotypes *are* the stories and symbolise a »›racialization‹ of brand identities«.[210]

3.1 Initial Campaigns

Established during World War I, the figure of Bonhomme Banania was not the first image used in product promotions. When Pierre-François Lardet first marketed his new breakfast cereal inspired by a »delightful exotic drink« he tasted in Nicaragua, his first choice for an advertisement figure was a »light skinned mulâtresse with a madras scarf and shawl [...] associating [the product] with the French Antilles«.[211] Arranged in a tropical surrounding in between banana trees, she visually poured out the gifts of Banania (vigour, health, energy, strength) on exultant French consumers and therewith represented initial suppositions of its curative effects and the alleged naturalness of the tropical colonies (fig. 34).[212]

207 Malte Hinrichsen: Promoting Racism, p. 262.
208 Wolfgang F. Haug: Critique of Commodity Aesthetics, pp. 49, 50.
209 Marie Hardin: Argument: Stereotypes are the best way to give consumers a quick understanding of the creative impact of the message, p. 130.
210 Anandi Ramamurthy: Imperial Persuaders, p. 15.
211 Brett A. Berliner: Ambivalent Desire, p. 10.
212 For the discourses on Banania's healthiness see Pierre Julien: Banania. Fig. 34: Charles Tichon, early Banania advertisement (1911), in Brett A. Berlin-

Fig. 34: Pouring the alleged gifts of Banania on the celebrating French public, the Antillaise was the first advertising figure of the cereal producer and symbolised the attractiveness of colonial fantasies.

As Dana Hale observes, prior to World War I, French marketers expressed exoticism with both African and Caribbean characters; however, blacks were still mostly displayed in a heraldic fashion, referring to the traditional stereotype of the moor. By the fin-de-siècle, this iconography dithered between »classical designs and caricatures« and already embraced comical elements and exaggerated features evoking connotations of American minstrelsy.[213] Until 1850, representations of blacks in French popular culture had been dominated by abolitionism and scientific discourses on racial inferiority and, consequently, offered »few examples of comic caricature«.[214] However, during the second half of the 19th century and with the success of minstrel shows, »racisme à l'Américaine« made its way to French visual culture and influenced racialised representations in advertising and other popular images (fig. 35).[215]

At the outset of World War I, French products were increas-

er: Ambivalent Desire.

213 Dana S. Hale: Races on Display, pp. 25-27.

214 Ardelle Striker: Spectacle in the Service of Humanity, p. 76.

215 »À l'origine, le Noir tête d'affiche est noir américain. Il apparaît à l'occasion des tournées qu'effectuèrent les minstrel's shows en France à partir de la seconde moitié du siècle dernier.«, Raymond Bachollet et al.: Négripub, p. 33; Marc Michel: L'image du soldat noir, p. 88. Fig. 35: Jules-Alexandre Grün, show poster (1904), in Raymond Bachollet et al.: Négripub.

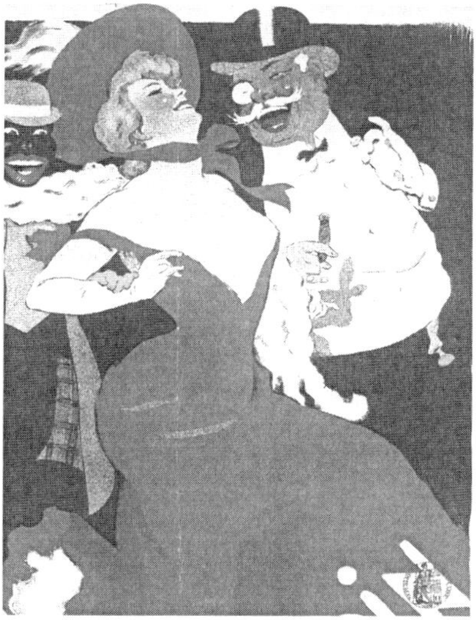

Fig. 35: American images of race from the fin-de-siècle onwards influenced French perceptions of blacks and resulted in comical representations in advertising and popular culture.

ingly promoted with »blatantly derogatory images«, featuring for example caricatural »black children and childlike adults in comic scenes«; a fact that Hale traces back to »American images of blacks in publications, posters, and trademarks for items sold in France«.[216] Around the same time, even black soldiers, although to a certain degree positively acknowledged by authorities, were belittled in popular representations and sometimes became subjects of demeaning caricatures and, thus, illustrated the prevalence of the savage stereotype in French popular culture.[217] Nevertheless, the first version of Bonhomme Banania, designed by Alexandre De Andreis in 1915, was rather realistic and, in the interpretation of Nederveen Pieterse, allows »identification with the viewer«, being »[a]mong European black types [...] the only figure who is or seems to be real [...] and the only one who is sympathetic without being an idiot«.[218]

However, as Anne Donadey argues against Nederveen Pieterse, since even the supposedly authentic »images [...] explicitly participate in a white supremacist ideology« they are, »caricatured or not, [...] part of commodity racism«.[219] It was after several

216 Dana S. Hale: Races on Display, p. 94, 97.
217 Cf. Ouriel Reshef: Guerre, mythes et caricature, pp. 175-176.
218 Jan Nederveen Pieterse: White on Black, p. 162.
219 Anne Donadey: ›Y'a bon Banania‹, p. 11.

»re-stylings« that the soldier »who was originally not a caricature, has become one«, as even the most lifelike images »depicted the stereotype of the bon noir or bon nègre« with childlike, carefree faces grinning to please the consumer.[220] According to Brett Berliner, »the Bonhomme's smile« makes for the »central element of De Andreis's poster« and »was not merely an artistic element emphasizing the darkness of his skin«. Referring to traditional frameworks of stereotyping, this laughter symbolised one side of the »nègres essence: the nègre was a happy child, and his emotions were limited to the simple naïve joy of a child«.[221] Thus, although not a political statement, the initial Banania campaigns did »play on important ideologies of the time«, influenced by aforementioned discourses on colonial troops and their service in World War I, and played a crucial role in diminishing anxieties about Africans stationed in Paris and other French cities.[222] Additionally, while the »benevolent, childlike nature« of Bonhomme Banania was suitable »in order to reassure French people«, even the ›negative‹ aspects of racial stereotypes like the »savage nature and warrior qualities« could be embraced because they were directed »against the German enemy«.[223]

Like many of the other Tirailleurs Sénégalais that were frequently used in advertising of that period, Bonhomme Banania was combined with the slogan »Y'a Bon« that »was borrowed from the uniformly obsequious answers Senegalese soldiers were said to give when questioned about living conditions in the French army: ›Y'a bon cuisine‹, ›Y'a bon capitaine‹, ›Y'a bon pinard‹« (fig. 36).[224] Underlining their supposed simplicity and childishness, »tirailleurs were only taught ›pidgin‹ French sufficient for them to comprehend and execute basic commands«.[225] It was this so-called ›petit-nègre‹ that exemplified the alleged »limited civili-

220 Jan Nederveen Pieterse: White on Black, p. 163; Dana S. Hale: Races on Display, p. 95.

221 Brett A. Berliner: Ambivalent Desire, p. 14.

222 Anne Donadey: ›Y'a bon Banania‹, p. 13. For visual representations of these discourses in French popular culture see various essays in Pascal Blanchard and Armelle Chatelier: Images et Colonies. For advertising in particular see Jean-Barthélemi Debost: La publicité lave plus blanc.

223 Anne Donadey: ›Y'a bon Banania‹, p. 14.

224 Dana S. Hale: Races on Display, p. 95; Susan J. Terrio: Crafting the Culture and History of French Chocolate, p. 250.

225 Joe Lunn: Memoirs of the Maelstrom, p. 107.

Fig. 36: During World War I, the slogan »Y'a bon« became a symbol for the simple-minded contentment of French colonial soldiers and was used in advertising for various products.

zation« of the Africans and later attracted the greater part of public criticism. At the time, however, the racist instruction policies of French authorities potentially enabled the ›grand enfant‹ stereotype to take on a life on its own by, possibly, forcing some of the soldiers, »unable to communicate well with the French, [to] smile [... their] way through the métropole«.[226]

Nevertheless, even images that infantilised and belittled the black soldiers soon became subjects of sexual controversies in the French public. Frequent comic images featured a »wounded Senegalese soldier with a French nurse in his arms« and, following the racist logic of these representations, even a »Catholic nun« could be »sexually activated by the dumbfounded but sexually naive African soldier« (fig. 37).[227] Since Banania was »targeting children as its main market, [...] images of tirailleurs could only be the most peaceful, asexual and non-threatening of representations« and,

226 Jan Nederveen Pieterse: White on Black, p. 163; Brett A. Berliner: Ambivalent Desire, p. 14. See an in-depth discussion of French racist linguistic politics towards colonial soldiers in Cécile Van den Avenne: Bambara et français-tirailleur. Fig. 36: Banania advertisement (1920), in Raymond Bachollet et al.: Négripub.

227 Peter Bloom: French Colonial Documentary, pp. 43-45. Fig. 37: French caricature (c.1914), in Sylvie Chalaye: Du Noir au nègre.

Fig. 37: French postcards and caricatures played on the taboo of miscegenation by representing colonial soldiers with white women.

thus, Bonhomme Banania was further emasculated after World War II by erasing the »body, leaving only his head, smile, chechia, and disembodied hand cradling a spoon along with the words ›Y'a bon‹«.[228] Removing the reference to the traditionally sexualised black body, now available to French women, further confirms the suspicion that Banania, against Nederveen Pieterse's reading, was never interested in authenticity. A later version of the Tirailleur with two bananas replacing limbs and torso is final evidence of the total lack of racial sensitivity (figs. 38-39).[229]

By the time the first Banania campaigns were launched in 1915, Sarotti in Germany had already witnessed a long and diverse history of marketing strategies. Founded in 1852 as confectionary »Felix & Sarotti«[230] in Berlin Friedrichstraße, their first advertisements had to be akin to official bulletins because market customs in mid-19th-century Prussia were still influenced by former guild culture and blatant promotion was considered vulgar and immor-

228 Anne Donadey: ›Y'a bon Banania‹, p. 14; Brett A. Berliner: Ambivalent Desire, p. 15.

229 Figs. 38 and 39: advertisements from 1936 and 1956, in Raymond Bachollet et al.: Négripub.

230 The origin of the name Sarotti is not exactly recorded, for some theories about it see Rita Gudermann: Der Sarotti-Mohr, pp. 12-13.

Figs. 38-39: Between the 1930s and 1950s the tirailleur lost his original ›authentic‹ appearance and became more caricatural, desexualised and servile.

al. Initially addressing bourgeois upper classes, founders Heinrich and Louis Neumann praised the exclusiveness of their assortment and, similar to Banania about 60 years later, referred to possible medical applications of their chocolates, which were »scientifically approved compounds«.[231] After pastry cook Hugo Hoffmann purchased the business in 1868, he established Sarotti as a brand name protected by the trademark law of 1874 and introduced a bee-surrounded bear looking for honey in a hive as the first visual symbol of the young company.[232]

Especially among new brands, elaborate promotion was used to justify higher prices and frequently referred to fashionable images of exoticism or colonial life.[233] The marketing of Sarotti, however, still oscillated between oriental representations (as applied at the

231 »[...] wissenschaftlich anerkannte Präparate [...]«, opening announcement of »Felix & Sarotti« in Vossische Zeitung (16.9.1852), cited in Rita Gudermann: Der Sarotti-Mohr, pp. 14-15. For German discourses on the healthiness of colonial produce see Annerose Menninger: Die Verbreitung von Schokolade, Kaffee, Tee und Tabak in Europa, pp. 29-30.

232 Rita Gudermann: Der Sarotti-Mohr, pp. 25, 35-36.

233 As one of the first companies in Germany, soup producer Liebig used trade cards with colonial and oriental motifs. Cf. Joachim Zeller: Bilderschule der Herrenmenschen.

Fig. 40: Referring to traditional black servants and the stereotype of the moor, Sarotti introduced the ›3-Mohren-Mischung‹ in 1918 and five years later established a single moor with a tray as the new trademark symbol.

1896 industrial exhibition in Berlin), modern references to dairy farming (used on the packages of chocolate bars around the turn-of-the-century), and colonial sceneries (as on trading cards from the early 1910s).[234] Thus, blacks were only marginally featured in Sarotti advertising until 1918, when graphic artist Julius Gipkens, on the occasion of the company's fiftieth birthday, was commissioned to design a new trademark symbol.[235] With the company now being situated on Mohrenstraße in Berlin and building upon the connotations of chocolate with blackness and Africa, Gipkens initially chose three black servants to decorate the »Drei-Mohren-Mischung«, which fit with the multiple moor figures being used in early 20th century German advertising (fig. 40).[236]

234 Rita Gudermann: Der Sarotti-Mohr, pp. 37-39, 46-47.

235 Rita Gudermann: Der Sarotti-Mohr, pp. 53-57. On some controversies about the history of origins of the first Sarotti-Mohr see Thomas Kleber: Der Sarotti-Mohr, pp. 61-62.

236 In the first years after the establishment of the Sarotti-Mohr as the company's trademark figure, there was still a variety of marketing strategies. These included the occurrence of black »Lotti«, princess of the chocolate land, in a promotional picture-book, who targeted children as customers and, made of »sugar, butter, milk and flour, raisins, almond and cinnamon«, directly referred to the tradition of ›edible blacks‹. Cf. Rita Gudermann: Der Sarotti-Mohr, p. 79. Fig. 40: chocolate box (1918), ibid.

Figs. 41-42: In the early 20th century, companies like Sarotti and Meinl introduced a moor as their trademark figure, trying to evoke fantasies of exoticism and luxury while building on the tradition of emblematic moors, as in the coat of arms of the Tucher family and brewery.

Since the 13th century, the Nuremberg family of Tucher wore a black figure on their coat of arms and applied it as a trademark symbol of »Tucher Bräu« after taking over a brewery in 1855.[237] Similarly, many pharmacies and taverns referred to the old ›Wappenmohren‹, and the Austrian coffee producer Meinl also established an orientally dressed black as its trademark figure shortly after Sarotti (figs. 41-42).[238] In its specific case, however, the Sarotti-Mohr was not merely representative of this tradition of the moor as an emblematic device but, with his caricatural physiognomy and inspiration later taken from a juvenile black actor, he also mirrored the influence of American culture on German perceptions of race.[239] Especially the success of the ›cakewalk‹, with

237 In 1512 the coat of arms was redrawn by Albrecht Dürer who himself had a moor in his personal emblem. Peter Martin: Schwarze Teufel, Edle Mohren, pp. 50-55.

238 Walter Sauer: Stereotypen der österreichisch-afrikanischen Begegnung, pp. 185-189. Fig. 41: trademark symbol of the Tucher brewery (1906), in Peter J. Bräunlein: Von Mohren-Apotheken und Mohrenkopf-Wappen; fig. 42: Meinl advertisement (1918), in Raymond Bachollet et al.: Négripub.

239 In the German reception of the Sarotti-Mohr his face is referred to as following a ›Kindchenschema‹. Without a doubt representing a childlike figure, however, it is misleading to neglect the racial connotations of his facial

its image of the »American Negro [as] a child of nature, and one of the most entertaining, interesting and happy of beings«, transmitted the minstrelised faces beyond the Atlantic.[240] »[O]riginally a plantation dance in which blacks parodied whites and their stiff forms of dance«, the cakewalk soon was turned into a European »nigger fashion« in which traditional prejudices and popular images coalesced into a commercialised stereotype of the black as a natural entertainer.[241]

Moreover, according to Rainer Lotz and Thomas Kleber, William McAllan, a black German actor that was later featured in the film version of Hauff's Orientalist fairytale *Der kleine Muck,* acted as a model for the Sarotti-Mohr after playing a servant in a silent film in 1920.[242] McAllan's anglicised alias is evidence of the predominant impact of the United States on the German movie-making industry. From the start, racial stereotyping was a primary ingredient of Atlantic popular culture, in which »the fool became an emancipator« or entertaining foolishness became the last resort to escape from slavery and oppression.[243] Likewise in Germany, blacks found a niche of supposed acceptance in film, but were either negatively depicted as savage Africans or ›positively‹ ridiculed as African-American coons.[244] By the time of the 1936 Olympics, black entertainers (in show and sport) were so closely linked to the U.S., that Joseph Goebbels, worrying about the international reputation of Germany, instructed the media in political correctness: »Negroes are American citizens and must be treated with respect as Americans«.[245]

However, despite his minstrelised face, the Sarotti-Mohr in his advertising application did not represent the foolish American »Sambo«. Looking at the example of an early ad from 1925, the

features. Cf. Rita Gudermann: Der Sarotti-Mohr, p. 58.

240 Brooke Baldwin: The Cakewalk, p. 205. See also Astrid Kusser: Cakewalking the Anarchy of Empire around 1900; and James Deaville: Cakewalk in Waltz Time?. On the nexus of the black's »natural rhythm« and American minstrel culture see Ronald Radano: Hot Fantasies.

241 Jan Nederveen Pieterse: White on Black, pp. 137-138.

242 Rainer E. Lotz: Black People, pp. 283-284; Thomas Kleber: Der Sarotti-Mohr, pp. 62-63.

243 Rainer E. Lotz: Black People, p. 148; Joseph Boskin: Sambo, p. 218.

244 Cf. Tobias Nagl: ›...und lass mich filmen und tanzen bloß um mein Brot zu verdienen‹.

245 Cited in United States Holocaust Memorial Museum: The Nazi Olympics, Berlin 1936.

Figs. 43-44: With only three years between the two publications, the Sarotti-Mohr illustrates the dualistic character of racism, as he innocently accompanies attractive women to the dressing room, while, at the same time, blacks were publicly accused of spreading venereal diseases and raping white women.

Sarotti-Mohr directly mirrors the European iconography of the black servant. Accompanying two attractive women to the dressing room and offering his chocolates on his mandatory tray, this image translated the eroticised harem servant for Weimar middle classes. The sexual connotations, or the lack of them, become especially surprising, when looking at other contemporary images of black men with white women, addressing the so-called »black shame« (figs. 43-44).[246] Frequently depicted in apelike appearance, black soldiers were accused of stealing and raping white women, allegedly spreading both venereal diseases and racial impurity. This fundamental complexity of the image of the Sarotti-Mohr within popular racism in Germany of the 1920s and 1930s is strikingly

246 This duality of stereotypical representations of blacks in German popular culture was already present during the German Empire and in the context of the Herero wars. Cf. Frank O. Sobich: »Schwarze Bestien, rote Gefahr«, pp. 137-139. Fig. 43: Sarotti advertisement (1925), in Rita Gudermann: Der Sarotti-Mohr; Fig. 44: Karl Arnold: Sanktionen (1922), in Peter Martin and Christine Alonzo (eds.): Zwischen Charleston und Stechschritt.

Fig. 45: Even during the racist Nazi-era, the corporate newspaper of Sarotti referred to the Sarotti-Mohr as virtually leading Germans to the battlefield.

illustrated by the fact that the author of Sarotti's first corporate history, Hans Macco, became one of the most prominent apologists of the forced sterilisation of so-called ›Rhineland Bastards‹ in the early days of the Third Reich.[247] Paradoxically, even during the racist Nazi era and in times of war, some of these dark-skinned children dressed as the Sarotti-Mohr in public parades and the Sarotti *Werkszeitung* propagated the moorish trademark figure as symbolically unifying the company's personnel and promoted total commitment for the ultimate military victory (fig. 45).[248] At the same time, blacks in Germany were long classified as »persons of alien blood«, stripped of citizenship and political rights and were »forced to leave Germany or suffer the consequences of being sent to a concentration camp«.[249]

Likewise complex, but of different characteristics, was the relationship between blacks as represented in advertising and their real positions in society in the United States. Since the late 19th century »overtly racialized depictions of American consumerism« had created an »ideal (white) [...] consumer« and a conception of the »United States as a specifically white, consumer nation«.[250] As one main strand of this depiction, the visual contrast of black

247 Cf. Hans Macco: Die Entstehungsgeschichte der Schokoladenfabrik Sarotti; id.: Rasseprobleme im Dritten Reich. Cf. Robert W. Kestling: Blacks under the Swastika, p. 89.

248 Rita Gudermann: Der Sarotti-Mohr, pp. 94-98. Fig. 45: Reprint from the Sarotti-Werkszeitung (1943), ibid.

249 Clarence Lusane: Hitler's Black Victims, pp. 106-107, 222.

250 Marilyn M. Mehaffy: Advertising Race / Raceing Advertising, p. 133.

(slave) production and white consumption constructed a »scene of domestic colonialism« with the »black labourer [...] as the regressive foil for both the (white) consumer and late-century civic ideals of U.S. technological innovation, and enlightened civilization«. Together with frequent depictions of black domestic servants, this dominant group of advertising images can be placed »in a larger national discourse – of plantation literature, the visual arts, and politics – mythologizing antebellum slavery as a more coherent, tranquil era ›lost‹ to the uncertainties and upheavals of postwar urbanism, industrialism, and commercialization«.[251]

The second group of popular advertising motifs featuring blacks in 19th century U.S. can be attributed to »ethnic humor« and included defamatory language and comical representations.[252] Also familiar in Europe, this category of depictions directly referred to traditional justifications of white supremacy and as it played »on connotations of the distinction black/white, such as clean/dirty, dark/light, it [got] at the foundations of racial thinking«.[253] Besides general humiliations as ›good-for-nothing coons‹, popular images surrounded the subjects of cannibalism and white-washing blacks. Thus, especially soap companies illustrated the cleaning power of their products with supposedly whitened blacks and also referred to the »macro-level of white supremacy« in claiming: »A clean nation has ever been a strong nation«.[254] But whereas this fashion of advertising slowly vanished over the course of the 20th century, the usage of black slaves and servants in promotional activities continued and, with the prominent face of Uncle Ben, reached global popularity.

As the company used to announce on its website, the »namesake, Uncle Ben, was an African-American rice grower who harvested his rice with such care that he reaped honors for the full kernel yields and quality«.[255] Since later rice-growers supposedly used the crops of this legendary farmer as the »standard by which all other rice was judged«, the company owners chose the name ›Uncle Ben's‹ to promote their product manufactured in a revo-

251 Marilyn M. Mehaffy: Advertising Race / Raceing Advertising, pp. 135-136, 142.
252 Marilyn Kern-Foxworth: Aunt Jemima, Uncle Ben, and Rastus, pp. 29-33.
253 Jan Nederveen Pieterse: White on Black, p. 195.
254 Malte Hinrichsen: Promoting Racism, p. 262; Marilyn M. Mehaffy: Advertising Race / Raceing Advertising, p. 143.
255 About Uncle Ben's.

lutionary process of conversion.[256] The substance of this alleged background story is unverifiable; however, to create a mythological foundation in the attempt to base a product's value on a true story was a widespread practice in early 20th century American advertising. Thus, the marketing of Aunt Jemima, a food company named after a stereotypical mammy figure, soon included stories about her life in a Southern mansion, which were published on napkins in the Aunt Jemima Restaurant and »became part of American folklore«.[257] Beyond the promised »domestic wisdom that transformed ordinary women into exceptional housewives«, the advertising exemplified the »centrality of antebellum idealism in America's developing consumer culture« and presented »value systems framed by the constant reminder that we live in a vibrantly successful capitalist society«.[258] As will be further examined in the following chapter, this is one incident that illustrates how advertising messages appeal to the emotions of customers and potentially interact with national historical narratives.

Like Aunt Jemima and the racialised products previously discussed (see chapter 2.3), the character of Uncle Ben, which »shrunk down over the years from a full-sized image [...] to a small oval at the top« of the box, truly bears some superficial connection to the food product he sells.[259] Michele Washington describes the usage of a black character as the trademark figure of food companies as a reference to an »ironic authority«, because »Aunt Jemima, Uncle Ben, and their offspring are experts in their ›fields‹ and that's what makes their products good«. However, as Washington observes, the mere title of an ›uncle‹ in combination with the lack of a surname reveals »a form of pseudo respect« towards the black, despite the fact that in real plantation society »an ›uncle‹ of Ben's caliber would have exactly been the most dependable authority on rice«.[260] Whereas this reading highlights the racist dimension of the figure, Katherine Parkin contradictorily suggests, with regards to gender roles, that Uncle Ben »was an expert rice farmer and advertisers traded on his reputation [... and] relied on the male

256 About Uncle Ben's; cf. Science: Richer Rice.
257 Marilyn Kern-Foxworth: Aunt Jemima, Uncle Ben, and Rastus, pp. 70-73.
258 Kimberly Wallace-Sanders: Mammy, pp. 67-68.
259 Jay P. Pederson: International Directory of Company Histories, p. 529.
260 Michele Y. Washington: Ironic Authority, pp. 43-45.

authority [...] to gain the confidence of consumers«.[261] Luckily, this controversy can be dissolved with a close look at the figure's image.

Readily identifiable in clothing and appearance, Uncle Ben is not merely evocative of rice farming, but in his tie and jacket rather represents a »waiter or a Pullman porter«, which integrates him in a whole range of images that connect romantic histories of slavery with American social realities of the 20th century.[262] Originally picturing Frank Brown, a »close friend« of the two founders and a »restaurant's maître d'«, the black man in a waiter's uniform on the rice boxes was not an unusual choice for advertising activities (figs. 46-47).[263] According to a 1969 survey by Harold Kassarjian, by the time Uncle Ben's was first promoted »78 percent of American Negro actors or models were depicted in the ads as having labourer or service jobs: maid, waiter, slave, field hand, personal servant«.[264] Especially after World War II, the »most persistent representations« remained »that of the Pullman porter, cook, or waiter«, but most of them, like the mammy types (except for Aunt Jemima), remained anonymous and disposable, and were frequently embodied by just a few black models.[265] However, like Uncle Ben, they combined »invented memories of loyal black houseslaves« that had been created in the early 20th century with the social realities of a segregated job market, where »nearly 65 percent of Black men and over 80 percent of Black women work[ed] as domestics and in personal services«, a figure that only slowly decreased towards mid-century.[266]

Even today, marketing experts perceive Uncle Ben's rice as an example of exceptional success in transforming a basic product into a recognizable trademark through advertising.[267] Similarly, the Sarotti-Mohr, being Germany's oldest existing trademark symbol,

261 Katherine J. Parkin: Food is Love, p. 132.
262 Katherine J. Parkin: Food is Love, p. 45.
263 Marilyn Kern-Foxworth: Aunt Jemima, Uncle Ben, and Rastus, p. 49. Figs. 46-47: advertisements for Pabst Beer (c. 1930) and Budd Trains (1945), in Michael S. Barnes: The Tom-Caricature.
264 Harold H. Kassarjian: The Negro and American Advertising, p. 35.
265 Elspeth H. Brown: Black models and the Invention of the US ›Negro Market‹, pp. 189-190; Maurice M. Manring: Slave in a Box, p. 116.
266 Elspeth H. Brown: Black models and the Invention of the US ›Negro Market‹, p. 193; Clovis E. Semmes: Racism, Health, and Post-Industrialism, p. 58.
267 Keith Brumfitt et al.: Vocational Business, p. 27.

Figs. 46-47: Waiters and Pullman porters were among the most persistent stereotypical roles for blacks in advertising. When overt racist ›humour‹ was long condemned, black servility was still a profitable feature of marketing and inspired the image of Uncle Ben.

in 2004 still reached a level of awareness of approximately 94 percent and, despite some financial problems, Banania, with its familiar posters, is still one of the best-known brands in France.[268] As Isabell Cserno argues, with reference to German and American racist advertising, most of the relevant »product campaigns emerge[d] at a time of complex social and economic changes as both Germany and the United States evolved as powerful nation-states with colonial and imperialist politics«.[269] Likewise, in the case of Banania, socio-economic evolution in France was accompanied by visual cultures that referred to traditional stereotypes of blacks and, thus, these ›fashionable‹ representations found entrance into the marketers' repertoire of popular advertising images.

However, even if it is proved that each of these three trademark figures built on the specific sets of ›positive‹ stereotypes that resulted from the individual national discourses on blackness, there are other old and prosperous brands, which never used racial im-

268 Hattersheimer Geschichtsverein 1985: Machbarkeitsstudie, p. 6; Sauveurs des marques.

269 Isabell Cserno: Race and Mass Consumption in Consumer Culture, abstract.

agery to merchandise their products. This raises the question of whether and to what extent the figures' inherent racism contributed to the products' success. This examination of the stereotypes' roles in consumer society will start with one common feature that illustrates the tangible influence of the racialised types: the figures were not just present on product packages and in direct advertising, but were soon included on merchandise items that were completely detached from the commodities' utility but still hugely successful among collectors in the different countries. Each of the figures became part of its society's popular culture and, with its individual popularity, both enabled and symbolised their respective companies' sustainable success.

3.2 Roles in Consumer Society

In European markets, like in the U.S., trading cards were established as a means of commercial advertising in the late 19th century and addressed particularly children as collectors and involuntary multipliers of the promotional messages.[270] In Germany, a meat extract producer called Liebig produced trading cards which resulted in »collecting-mania« and encouraged the company to expand their marketing to England, Italy and France. Looking for motifs that were applicable to »these very different national cultures, and yet [...] inoffensive to all [...], [c]olonial themes offered one solution«.[271] With the single target of increasing the brand's popularity, Liebig's built on the human desire to structure the world through collecting, and on traditional representations of Africa, suggesting a cultural hierarchy in favour of Europe and the so-called Western World.

Similar patterns can be identified in the marketing campaigns of Sarotti, Banania, and Uncle Ben's. Since an advertisement's purpose is always to sell a product, the marketers searched for images that were commonly appealing to the (white) target customers and discovered that consumers still maintained a fascination with the Other depicted in servile, childlike and obsequious fashion, while reflecting specific national discourses on blackness.[272]

270 Cf. Knut Hickethier: Wundertüten, Überraschungseier, Sammelbilder, p. 32. See also Joachim Zeller: Bilderschule der Herrenmenschen.

271 David Ciarlo: Advertising Empire, pp. 184-185.

272 Cf. Jean-Barthélemi Debost: La publicité lave plus blanc, p. 97.

Whereas Liebig's trading cards explicitly told stories of colonial life, the three brands listed above relied on the implicit stories of race and social structure inherent in the smiling faces of the trademark figures, which were allotted central roles in their promotional activities. While they all referred to a traditional notion of the good savage that resulted from centuries of racial discourses and constituted one side of the dualistic character of racial othering, each figure had a different message for the respective consumer society:[273] Uncle Ben reassured the American public of possible racial harmony and, likewise, referred to Southern mythologies of antebellum times and to romantic racialist perceptions of the black as the benevolent child; the Sarotti-Mohr similarly promoted the luxury of being served, but was iconographically based on classic European perceptions of exoticised black servants, shaped by contact with Islam and still attractive to the German public at a time when French colonial troops were being demonised in the media for their racial inferiority; Bonhomme Banania, representing these soldiers, developed his innocent image in conflict with the barbaric ›boches‹, in which all aggressiveness and violence was removed and only the most trustful and friendly traits remained on boxes and posters. How these messages were transmitted and, to a certain degree, detached from the commodities' utility values in social environments of deeply entrenched racisms will be the subject of the following examination.

As early as the 1920s, Sarotti started to produce dolls of the Sarotti-Mohr in materials ranging from plaster to porcelain to glass to cloth. Time and again, until the 1980s, they put out limited editions of collection figures that realised prices up to several thousand German Marks in various markets.[274] Similar sums are still offered for comparable Banania objects on the francophone internet, where collectors proudly present their accumulations and desperately search for missing pieces.[275] Even though Uncle Ben did not materialise beyond regular advertising activities to this extent, the United States is the birthplace of collecting black memorabilia,

273 For the »double aspect« of racial stereotypes see Anne Donadey: ›Y'a bon Banania‹, pp. 13-14.

274 Volker Ilgen and Dirk Schindelbeck: Jagd auf den Sarotti-Mohr, pp. 29-30.

275 See for example http://bananiaphile.free.fr/index.htm; http://www.banania.c.la/; http://banania.chez.com/index.htm.

with mammy and uncle figures as the most notorious artefacts.[276] Thus, the independent celebrity of the three products' figureheads indicates their impact on the commercial success of their respective products; however, their functions as collectibles have further implications for their promotional values.

Tracing back the origins of collecting, the starting point can be found at the cradle of modern racist thinking: the European Enlightenment of the 18th century. Simultaneous to the quest for a natural order and the early constructions of frameworks for all existing phenomena, which eventually resulted in the abovementioned racial hierarchies, upper-class Europeans of the 17th and 18th centuries developed the »almost ubiquitous conviction that objects could say things« and Lord Kames, among others, believed that through collecting objects one could »make a regular chain of causes and effects«.[277] For French philosopher Jean Baudrillard »collecting is a rudimentary way of mastering the outside world« and, similarly, »other collectors imagine the past through their hobby«.[278] In this context, black collectibles emerged in the American »post-Reconstruction era« as stereotypical references to the times of slavery and, in addition to the genuine psychological functions of collecting, »the fixity of the stereotype [...] compensate[d] for the new heterogeneity of black America [... and] for uncertainties about the future place and role of African American Americans in the U.S.« With these objects finding »a considerable European market« and since »manufacturers in Germany, [and] France [...] found significant domestic markets for their own black objects«, it was only a matter of time before marketers on both sides of the Atlantic discovered the value of stereotypical collectibles for their advertising activities.[279]

As Stacey Baker, Carol Motley and Geraldine Henderson have shown in two insightful studies of black advertising memorabilia in the U.S., »marketing materials with stereotypical depictions of African Americans have played a major role in the framing

276 Cf. Kenneth W. Goings: Mammy and Uncle Mose; Elvin Montgomery: Collecting African American History.

277 Susan M. Pearce: On Collecting, p. 114; cited in Christopher J. Berry: The Social Theory of the Scottish Enlightenment, p. 67.

278 Jean Baudrillard: The System of Objects, p. 93; John Bloom: Cardboard Patriarchy, p. 71.

279 Bill Brown: Reification, Reanimation, and the American Uncanny, pp. 186-187.

and understanding of American culture« and that the »manner in which African Americans were portrayed [...] provides a provocative context to demonstrate how collective memories and social values are constructed«.[280] In addition, Bill Brown shows, with the example of slavery, that »when and where it is no longer possible for a person to be a slave [...], we nonetheless find, in the post-history of that moment, residues of precisely that possibility«.[281] Conversely, whites who were no longer in the position of (potential) slaveholders, through this objectification of blacks could still consume their social and racial superiority.[282]

Among these black collectibles there were »few strictly decorative items« but rather most of them could »perform common service tasks« (such as salt and pepper shakers), underlining the servile role of the caricatured blacks (fig. 48).[283] Likewise, the collectibles were »almost universally derogatory, with exaggerated features that helped to ›prove‹ that, indeed, African-Americans were not only different but inferior as well«.[284] Although Uncle Ben's did participate in the business of black memorabilia and, in 1993, »made a collectible tin to celebrate the product's fiftieth anniversary«, the most common figures were anonymous representations of stereotypical black characters.[285] Nevertheless, uncle figures, frequently called ›Uncle Mose‹ after the husband of Aunt Jemima in early campaigns for Quaker Oats, have since the early 20th century occupied a space in American households that Uncle Ben's marketing could dovetail with.[286] It is partly due to this cultural breeding ground that Uncle Ben's »became an American icon and today is one of the most famous brands in the world«[287].

Especially after World War II, when television spots and wide-

280 Carol M. Motley, Geraldine R. Henderson and Stacey M. Baker: Exploring Collective Memories Associated with African-American Advertising Memorabilia, p. 55; id.: From Despicable to Collectible, p. 48.

281 Bill Brown: Reification, Reanimation, and the American Uncanny, p. 182.

282 In this context, Brown and others refer to the Marxist concept of »Versachlichung«. See also Michael A. Chaney: Fugitive Vision, pp. 206-208.

283 Steven C. Dubin: Symbolic Slavery, p. 123. Fig. 48: salt and pepper shakers depicting Aunt Jemima and Uncle Mose, in Kenneth W. Goings: Mammy and Uncle Mose.

284 Kenneth W. Goings: Mammy and Uncle Mose, p. xiii.

285 Dawn E. Reno: The Encyclopedia of Black Collectibles, p. 86.

286 Steven C. Dubin: Symbolic Slavery, p. 129. See also Kenneth W. Goings: Mammy and Uncle Mose, pp. xxiii-xiv.

287 Gary J. Allen and Ken Albala: The Business of Food, p. 375.

spread printed advertisings resulted in him becoming even more ubiquitous in German commodity culture, the Sarotti-Mohr was systematically merchandised beyond his company's core products.[288] On cups and cans, as key pendants and porcelain figurines, the famous black servant became buyable and received »honoured places in German living rooms« (fig. 49).[289] Still depicted as a classical black servant and waiting on women in everyday situations, he not only delivered pieces of chocolate, but also illusions of an ideal world and racial harmony, whereas blacks in post-war Germany were in reality still far from being accepted.[290] Afro-German Helga Emde, for example, remembers the Sarotti-Mohr as being »as well known as the Mercedes star« in the 1950s and as being the only possible disguise to wear in a »Mardi Gras parade« in order not to remind the audience of the »mulatto question«.[291] Thus, by surviving even the »race fanaticism of the National Socialists« and later controversies about German ›non-white‹ populations, the Sarotti-Mohr secured the deep entrenchment of his positive image.

The image of Bonhomme Banania, by contrast, who had always been successfully merchandised, »no longer worked so well [...] [o]nce he became the symbol of an immigrant population resident on French soil« following the independence of former African colonies in the 1950s. Thus, in France, it was not only the criticism from social movements (see ch. 3.3) that led to the original marketing figure becoming »progressively stylized, abstract, [...] incidental to the marketing of the product«, and temporarily disappearing in 1977.[292] At a time when Etienne Balibar and Pierre-André Taguieff diagnosed the breakthrough of a new form of racism that embraced resentments against all kinds of immigrants, a black soldier was no longer a promising advertising motif.[293] Against all

288 Rita Gudermann: Der Sarotti-Mohr, pp. 114-117.

289 Cf. Joachim Zeller: Bilderschule der Herrenmenschen, p. 223. Fig. 49: porcelain figurine of the Sarotti-Mohr, in Rita Gudermann: Der Sarotti-Mohr.

290 Thomas Kleber: Der Sarotti-Mohr, p. 77. For postwar Sarotti advertising see especially the television ads on http://www.sarotti.de/#/sarotti/markengeschichte/2006_1/ [05.09.2011]. Find a discussion of institutionalised racism after 1945 in Heide Fehrenbach: Afro-German Children and the Social Politics of Race after 1945.

291 Helga Emde: I too Am German, p. 35.

292 Susan J. Terrio: Crafting the Culture and History of French Chocolate, pp. 250-251.

293 Find the concepts of ›neo-racism‹ or ›differentialist racism‹ elaborated in

Figs. 48-49: Racist memorabilia and merchandising articles, featuring the racialised trademark figures, detached their subtle messages from the products and made them available in isolation.

odds, however, Banania memorabilia was cultivated in France and the »Senegalese tirailleur moved off the Banania box and posters and onto the daily breakfast table pitchers and mugs«.[294]

As early as the 1920s, France could have been described in the words of Laura Rice as a »Banania republic«, where images of the grinning black soldier »appeared on everything from food products to postcards joking about the barbarism of the African soldier, to manuals used in World War II to teach Senegalese troops to distinguish good from evil«.[295] Similarly, Peter Bloom refers to the interwar period in France as the »Banania years«, due to the »unprecedented proliferation of colonial imagery« with its famously grinning flagship symbol branding the »European and African imagination«.[296] Since the launch of the childlike Banania figure in 1915 the »company did much to cultivate this representation of blacks« and »not only plastered walls with the Bonhomme poster but also disseminated cartoon strip advertisements«.[297] And whereas, due to a »policy of blanchissement«, it took until 1994 to erect a statue to »commemorate the colonial units that helped

Etienne Balibar and Immanuel Wallerstein: Race, Nation, Class, pp. 17-28; and Pierre-André Taguieff: The Force of Prejudice, esp. pp. 200-208.

294 Leora Auslander and Thomas C. Holt: Sambo in Paris, p. 158.

295 Laura Rice: African Conscripts/European Conflicts, p. 121-122.

296 Peter Bloom: French Colonial Documentary, p. 43.

297 Brett A. Berliner: Ambivalent Desire, p. 14.

liberate France in 1944«, portraits and effigies of Bonhomme Banania and other black stereotypes have been ubiquitous features in French city life for nearly a century.[298]

As Leora Auslander and Thomas Holt demonstrate, these public representations of blacks often had »a clearly American referent«, so that the French public was familiar with genuine French images of the childlike colonial soldier, but also with »so-called mammies, Uncle Toms, dandies, and pickaninnies«.[299] Similarly, Isabell Cserno compares German popular culture, in which »any kind of cultural artefact with the Sarotti-Mohr on it has become a valuable item«, with the American passion for »›contemptible collectibles‹ such as Aunt Jemima cookie jars or postcards with pickaninnies«.[300]Like the way that European racist imagery and, consequently, racial trademark stereotypes have been widely influenced since the late 19th century by U.S. American minstrel shows, the second half of the 20th century was marked by an increasing universality of commodity racism. And again it is the American way of representing racialised products that proves internationally successful. Especially Uncle Ben's European campaigns, with their explicit references to *Uncle Tom's Cabin* and the associated stereotypes, exemplified the applicability of this specific American figure in foreign markets (fig. 50).[301]

It probably comes as no real surprise that in a century that was culturally dominated by products and publications from the United States, American representations of blacks can be found all around the world, whereas popular European stereotypes like Bonhomme Banania and the Sarotti-Mohr are unknown even in the bordering countries.[302] This fact reveals something about international and national patterns of anti-black racism: since the times of abolitionism and the unprecedented success of *Uncle Tom's Cabin,* Europe has been affected by the »globalization of America's home-grown

298 Brett A. Berliner: Ambivalent Desire, pp. 35-36.

299 Leora Auslander and Thomas C. Holt: Sambo in Paris, pp. 152, 159.

300 Isabell Cserno: Pancakes, Chocolate, and the Trap of Eternal Servitude, p. 69.

301 Raymond Bachollet et al.: Négripub, p. 83. Fig. 50: Uncle Ben's advertisement in France (1984), ibid.

302 The unprecedented rise of the United States to a economically, militarily and culturally dominating superpower, especially in the period after World War II, is examined in James T. Patterson: Grand Expectations.

Fig. 50: In contrast to the German and French companies that were using racial stereotypes, Uncle Ben's was able to wage international campaigns and rely on the universality of the image of the contented slave.

racism«.[303] Beginning in the 19th century, Europeans engaged in transatlantic debates, adopted stereotypes that were shaped in slave societies overseas and celebrated the racialised cultural exports of the United States. White Americans, of course, built their racist beliefs on the European spadework of the early modern and Enlightenment periods, but developed images of blacks in relative isolation from, for example, European discourses on colonialism and the Orient.

Considering these patterns, it is not surprising that the European figures of Sarotti and Banania, although the best-known black figures of their respective countries, are too closely related to specific national discourses to be applied internationally. American-based Uncle Ben's, however, could bank on a universal notion of the contented slave, given that docility and benevolence, although perhaps with different connotations, were inscribed in

303 Larry A. Greene: Race in the Reich, p. 81.

international stereotypes of blacks. While racial stereotypes became even more universal in the course of the 20th century, it was at the same time that blacks in Germany, France and the United States publicly advocated a critical perspective on their roles in society and started to fight against humiliating representations.[304] In particular the most conspicuous manifestastions of everyday racism came under the fire of social movements; however, even the possession of racist memorabilia could trigger a form of protest.

Collecting black figures and dolls is not always a conscious or unconscious consumption of traditional racist beliefs. Many collectors are blacks who view collecting as a means to the »development and continuance of positive self-esteem« or as a way to cope with racist humiliations of the past.[305] David Pilgrim, founder and curator of the Jim Crow Museum of Racist Memorabilia at Ferris State University in Michigan, describes himself as »a garbage collector, racist garbage« and uses his collection to inform about and prevent further racist representations.[306] When in the 1990s the demand for black memorabilia exploded, this was explained by Lynn Casmier-Paz partly by the »changed images and revised representations« in advertising: public »[r]acist images were beginning to disappear [... and] [f]or African American collectors [...] it became important that racist images become the property of African Americans«.[307] Another black collector justifies his interest by stating that »The souls of millions of black people were trapped in these heaps of mass-produced junk. Now at least they are being set free.«[308]

On the contrary, Micki McElya asserts that with the 1990s and the »sudden swell in the popularity of [...] racist material culture [...] [t]he faithful slave narrative has made a full terrible circle«.[309] Without a doubt, the 20th century witnessed a change in the perception of stereotypes, and social movements and anti-racism influenced popular representations of race in the United States as well as in Germany and France. In each of these countries, the

304 A summary of the origins and developments of postcolonialism and international anti-racism can be found in Cheryl McEwan: Postcolonialism and Development, esp. pp. 34-76.
305 Debbie B. Garrett: Black Dolls.
306 David Pilgrim: The Garbage Man.
307 Lynn Casmier-Paz: Heritage, not Hate?, pp. 48-49.
308 Kenneth W. Goings: Mammy and Uncle Mose, p. xxiv.
309 Micki McElya: Clinging to Mammy, p. 260.

three ubiquitous racial trademark figures discussed previously have been major subjects of public criticism. How this critique was articulated and whether the companies' reactions were sufficient to ›democratise‹ their racist icons will be discussed in the following chapter.

3.3 Critique and Reaction

Referring to the ideals of the French Revolution and the Declaration of the Rights of Man, wide parts of the French public believe that there is »a form of anti-racism that is rooted in French society and is part of French tradition«.[310] As President Georges Pompidou clarified after »a series of racist murders« in 1973, France, more than any other Western nation, understands itself as »profoundly antiracist«.[311] Especially for inhabitants of the colonies, this alleged colour blindness, paradoxically, constituted an obstacle in the fight for emancipation.[312] Thus, anti-colonialism could not simply refer to ›traditional‹ French anti-racism but had to come up with an active black self-awareness to challenge the racist reality of the Empire. As Jean-Paul Sartre described the programme of the so-called negritude, in his introduction to an anthology of African and West Indian poems edited by Leopold Senghor: »The negro cannot [...] claim that he is part of some abstract colorless humanity: he is black. [...] The unity which will come eventually [...] must be preceded by [...] the moment of separation or negativity: this anti-racist racism is the only road that will lead to the abolition of racial differences«.[313]

With Bonhomme Banania, the most visible black figure in French popular culture was a common target of anti-racists and anti-colonists, combining in his stereotypical appearance the clear reference to colonial exploitation and characteristics of racist ideologies. When Frantz Fanon emphasised the role of Banania among all racist attributions he had to endure in colonial France, it

310 Alastair Bonnett: Anti-Racism, p. 54.

311 Cited in Catherine Lloyd: Discourses of Antiracism in France, p. 1.

312 Even recent studies show that, for example, »Antillean activists in metropolitan France tend not to refer to race when formulating claims concerning identity«, cf. David Beriss: Culture-as-Race or Culture-as-Culture, p. 112.

313 Jean-Paul Sartre: Black Orpheus, p. 18. The Original essay, entitled ›Orphée Noir‹, was published in Leopold S. Senghor: Anthologie de la nouvelle poésie nègre et malgache de langue français.

was not incidental that mocked language (›Y'a bon‹) was a focus point. In the first chapter of *Black Skin, White Masks* he describes the importance of language for the colonised French in Martinique: »the Antilles Negro who wants to be white will be the whiter as he gains greater mastery of the cultural tool that language is.«[314] Conversely, as stated by Gobineau in the mid-19th-century, language in France has long been racially constricted to its ›natural‹ speakers: »when a language of a higher order is used by some human group which is unworthy of it, it will certainly become mutilated and die out«.[315] Thus, petit nègre, a »French African pidgin dialect« was imposed not just on colonial soldiers as the »major vehicular language« but was also used in public representations of blacks, such as comic strips and movies.[316] However, even though language was the first racist feature to be addressed in advertising and, indeed, as soon as »›parler petit nègre‹ was no longer bon ton, the ›Y'a bon‹ was dropped« by Banania's marketers, the words were definitely not the only focus of French postcolonial activism.[317]

When French poet Leopold Senghor cited the German scientist Leo Frobenius, »along with ›Louis Armstrong's trumpet‹ and ›Josephine Baker's hips‹, as inspiration to black students in Paris that their culture was different from but no less valid than French culture«, it earned him criticism from other black intellectuals, but also revealed the influence of German anthropology on the negritude movement.[318] Frobenius and most of his colleagues, however, supported colonial projects and, although they progressively acknowledged the existence of »African innovations in art, metallurgy, mining technology, [and] indigenous systems of ethics and morality«, their writings were »obfuscated with [...] patronizing and racist misconceptions«.[319] In Germany, up until the post-war era, overt everyday racism was ever-present and »Sarotti-Mohr«

314 Frantz Fanon: Black Skin White Masks, p. 29.
315 Cited in Laura Rice: Of Irony and Empire, p. 57.
316 Peter Bloom: French Colonial Documentary, p. 41; Frantz Fanon: Black Skin White Masks, p. 26.
317 Jan Nederveen Pieterse: White on Black, p. 163.
318 Andrew Zimmerman: Anthropology and Antihumanism in Imperial Germany, p. 246.
319 Matthias Fiedler: Zwischen Abenteuer, Wissenschaft und Kolonialismus, pp. 258-259; Jacob K. Olupona: A Tale of Two Germans and the Yoruba of Nigeria, p. 188.

was a common insult towards black citizens.[320] Moreover, in continuity to racial politics of the National Socialists, partners and offspring of black soldiers, in particular, were stigmatised when »West German federal and state Interior Ministry officials constructed the postwar problem of race around skin color and, even more narrowly, blackness«.[321]

Whereas the anti-black atmosphere of the early 20th century never interfered with the successful market presence of Sarotti's racialised icon, the emergence of anti-colonialist activism during the German student protest movement of the late 1960s eventually led to sustainable changes in the perception of Africans, which eventually became problematic for the company.[322] The identification of colonialist monuments as »manifestations of German attitudes of superiority and ruthlessness against other races that had led [...] to the catastrophe of the Holocaust« challenged traditions of racial representations and initiated discourses on linguistic and visual racisms in the Federal Republic of Germany.[323] Additionally, the American occupation and its racially-charged language induced changes in German designations of blacks and established an early notion of ›political correctness‹.[324] While in the 1950s, the term ›Neger‹ was almost the only label used for blacks in Germany, in the 1960s, the word ›Farbiger‹ was more frequently used, as ›Neger‹ had acquired an explicitly negative connotation.[325] Following the example of the American civil rights movement, organisations of blacks in Germany propagated a sensible language use and the self-designations of minorities gradually became accepted as appropriate diction, while traditional expressions including ›Mohr‹ were increasingly condemned.[326]

Beginning with black abolitionism and the Harlem Renaissance

320 Katharina Oguntoye, May Opitz and Dagmar Schultz: Farbe bekennen, p. 105.

321 Heide Fehrenbach: Black Occupation Children and the Devolution of the Nazi Racial State, p. 38.

322 Cf. Ingo Cornils: Denkmalsturz.

323 Ingo Cornils: Denkmalsturz, p. 197;

324 An interpretation and historical analysis of ›political correctness‹ can be found in Geoffrey Hughes: Political Correctness.

325 Martin Wengeler: Von der Hilfe für unterentwickelte Gebiete über den Neokolonialismus bis zur Entwicklungszusammenarbeit, p. 707.

326 Sabine Wierlemann: Political Correctness in den USA und in Deutschland, p. 195.

of the 1920s, blacks in the U.S. were engaged in a struggle for social participation and against slavery and the Jim Crow legislation. Politically, however, it took until the Montgomery Bus Boycott of 1955 and the strategy of civil disobedience for their organisations to become heard on a nationwide scale.[327] From the early 1960s, activists critically addressed the American advertising industry demanding »to have blacks represented [...] more frequently and in a nonracist manner«, especially focusing on two ubiquitous images: »the derogatory depiction of the African American woman as Aunt Jemima and of the African American man as Uncle Ben«.[328] Especially the former was publicly »transformed« by black artists to make »distinct political statements[...], deconstructing the visual sign, questioning Aunt Jemima's role as a popular trademark, and giving voice and humanity to all the black women aggrieved by the stereotypical representation« (fig. 51).[329]

While in the 1940s and 1950s, Uncle Ben's »brand awareness arose by cultivating associations between the brand [...] and intangible values (homeliness, friendliness)«, the product's eponym was »relegated to a minor role in the marketing« for most of the second half of the 20th century.[330] During this time, as a result of racial sensitivity, »many negative and demeaning stereotypical portrayals of African-Americans [...] largely disappeared«, or, at least, »changed in character, taking subtler and more symbolic or underhanded forms«.[331] However, despite all opposition, the figure of Uncle Ben remained prominent on the packaging and in the name, and his image, along with the images of select black trademark figures like »Aunt Jemima and the Cream of Wheat chef were redesigned and kept up, but in the unusual status of silent spokescharacters, removed from ads and reduced to staring mutely from packages«.[332]

327 For a history of the African American civil rights movement see Kevern Verney: The Debate on Black Civil Rights in America.

328 Daniel Horowitz: The Anxieties of Affluence, p. 178.

329 Michael D. Harris: Colored Pictures, p. 107. Examples of Aunt Jemima depicted with arms and virtually escaping the pancake box can be found in ibid., pp. 107-124. Fig. 51: Murry N. DePillars: Aunt Jemima (1968), reprinted ibid.

330 Mark Paterson: Consumption and Everyday Life, p. 205; Stuart Elliott: Uncle Ben, Board Chairman.

331 Julia M. Bristor, Renée G. Lee and Michelle R. Hunt: Race and Ideology, p. 50; Anthony J. Cortese: Provocateur, p. 91.

332 Stuart Elliott: Uncle Ben, Board Chairman.

Fig. 51: From the 1960s onwards, artists supporting the civil rights movement tried to break racial stereotypes and subverted the most visible derogatory representations such as Aunt Jemima.

Still facing public criticism at the beginning of the 21st century, for example by Jamaican-American artist Renée Cox, Uncle Ben's new owner Mars, Inc. decided to take offensive action and attempted to give the »bow-tied black figure [...] an ethnically sensitive makeover«.[333] In a 2007 campaign including a redesigned website, Uncle Ben is »reborn as Ben, an accomplished businessman with an opulent office, a busy schedule, an extensive travel itinerary and a penchant for sharing what the company calls his ›grains of wisdom‹ about rice and life« (fig. 52).[334] »As an African-American, he makes me feel so proud«, said Mars executive Vincent Howell as he expressed his feelings and, perhaps even stronger, his sought-after reception of the icon now presented »in a position of prominence and authority«.[335] In fact, there were many »positive responses to the elimination of a black figure as a servant and his reemergence as a successful businessman«, but taking into

333 Nikki L. M. Brown and Barry M. Stentiford: The Jim Crow Encyclopedia, p. 10; Andrew Clark: Uncle Ben promoted to the board.

334 Stuart Elliott: Uncle Ben, Board Chairman. Fig. 52: Uncle Ben's advertisement (2007), ibid.

335 Cited in Stuart Elliott: Uncle Ben, Board Chairman.

Fig. 52: Unaltered in face and appearance, but now representing a board chairman in his office, (Uncle) Ben was redesigned in 2007.

account that a »cosmetic improvement [...] cannot make up for the image's longer history of racist symbolism«, critics of the new makeover prevailed.[336]

Although now advertised with the claim »Ben knows best«, the company name still reveals the slavish past in the »decidedly unbusinesslike honorific« of ›Uncle‹. Howard Buford, a »real-life black leader of a company«, remarks: »rarely do you have someone of that stature addressed by his first name« – and without any hint of a surname.[337] Additionally, as Michele Washington notes, the »style makers failed to erase his royal blue jacket and crisp white shirt and dowdy bow tie – cultural expressions still linking him to his past as a waiter or Pullman porter«.[338] Similarly, Marilyn Kern-Foxworth, although »applaud[ing] them for the effort«, criticises the company's continuity of representation, which shows that »they're trying so hard to hold onto something I'm trying so

336 Nikki L. M. Brown and Barry M. Stentiford: The Jim Crow Encyclopedia, p. 10.

337 Nikki L. M. Brown and Barry M. Stentiford: The Jim Crow Encyclopedia; citation from Stuart Elliott: Uncle Ben, Board Chairman.

338 Michele Y. Washington: Ironic Authority, p. 45.

hard to get rid of«. When manager Howell summarises the consumer reception of the transformation as being »focused on positive images, quality, warmth, timelessness, [...] the legend of Uncle Ben«, this might reveal something about persistent racism in the U.S., but it definitely illustrates the connotations the company sought to revive by shedding supposedly new light on a figurehead that was nearly doomed to fade away.[339]

Just three years before Uncle Ben experienced his symbolic reevaluation, Sarotti in Germany, also under the influence of a new parent company, redesigned their controversial trademark image, although »you have to look twice to perceive the new in this traditional and familiar figure«.[340] Depicted in profile and still wearing a turban and exotic poulaines, the original Sarotti-Mohr is clearly referenced in the figure now called »Sarotti Magier der Sinne« (»Sarotti magician of the senses«) (fig. 53).[341] But instead of holding a tray or waving a flag, the figure is juggling with sparkling stars, which match the golden complexion that is substituting for the darkness of his servile predecessor. In commercials following the redesign, however, this allegedly de-racialised figure takes white consumers along to an Oriental fairyland, where black servants offer chocolate and luxury – all accompanied by exotic sounds.

Similar to the development of Uncle Ben's marketing, Sarotti since the 1970s increasingly did not use their figurehead's popularity in advertising activities, except for occasional vintage editions that sizably featured the moor with all his colonial and racial connotations.[342] Despite this absence, however, the Sarotti-Mohr remained the best-known and the most popular German trademark figure, a fact that led the company to allow him a prominent ›comeback‹ in 2004.[343] Despite all attempted political correctness

339 Cited in Stuart Elliott: Uncle Ben, Board Chairman.

340 »Man muss zweimal hinsehen, um das Neue an dieser alten, uns so wohl vertrauten Figur wahrzunehmen«, Joachim Zeller: Der magische Sarotti-Mohr, p. 28.

341 http://www.sarotti.de/#/sarotti/markengeschichte/2004_1/ [10.09.2011]. Fig. 53: Sarotti advertisement (2004), in Joachim Zeller and Heiko Wegmann: ›Mohren‹.

342 Dorothea Jung: Politische Literatur.

343 »Er ist die beliebteste deutsche Werbefigur – und auch die bekannteste. Bei 98 Prozent der Deutschen ruft der Sarotti-Mohr süße Erinnerungen wach.«, Dorothea Jung: Politische Literatur.

Fig. 53: The metamorphosis of the Sarotti-Mohr reveals continuity in visual language, with the exoticism of the turban and the Oriental symbols becoming more dominant to the skin colour, which eventually became gold.

in name and image, the company could not conceal that they were hoping for a reanimation of the figure's fame from the 1950s. Thus, they announced just two years after ›white-washing‹ the moor, that in particular commercials »the magician revives the tradition of the animatic moor«.[344] In addition, an affiliate company of Sarotti continued to play on the sexual connotations of ›white‹ and ›black‹ when they launched a new chocolate in 2009 called »Weisse Damen« (white ladies), which was meant to accompany the successful »Schwarze Herren« (black men) bars.[345] Although not advertised with the Sarotti-Mohr figure or his antecedent, this product, like Sarotti's marketing, illustrates the prevailing recklessness in dealing with traditional racial stereotypes.

Meanwhile in France, Bonhomme Banania underwent a real odyssey of transformation in reaction to continuous critique and, unlike Uncle Ben and the Sarotti-Mohr, a rise of overt racism in the 1970s, when »African Others [...] were reconceived as a social and economic problem«. Initially the figure was abstracted and reduced to an image showing just the head, hands and slogan; shortly afterwards the pidgin catchphrase was dropped and in 1977 the image of the African soldier was »removed [...] and replaced with

344 »Der Sarotti Magier lässt die Tradition des Zeichentrick-Mohren wieder aufleben: als Ansager für Kindersendungen.«, http://www.sarotti.de/#/sarotti/markengeschichte/2006_1/ [10.09.2011].

345 http://www.schwarze-herren-schokolade.de/ [04.09.2011].

Figs. 54: From the 1970s to the new millennium, the Tirailleur vanished from the packaging of Banania until he returned in the early 2000s. Still earning criticism, the company launched a rejuvenated edition with fez and smile referring to the ›grand enfant‹ of French colonial propaganda.

the symbol of postwar prosperity, population growth, and natural regeneration – the face of a rosy-cheeked, smiling child«.[346] However, similar to Uncle Ben and the Sarotti-Mohr, Bonhomme Banania's removal did not last long. In the early 2000s, Banania reinstalled the Tirailleur on their products' boxes in a version that, as Dana Hale notices, bears a remarkable historical significance: »ironically, the recycled African soldier image on the new boxes was first used in 1959, a date that marked the end of the French empire in Sub-Saharan Africa«.[347]

Nevertheless, this revival of the black trademark figure did not mark the end of Banania's controversial marketing. Being, once again, confronted with critical reactions, Banania decided to subject their figurehead to a rejuvenation and in 2005 they launched new packaging designs featuring a black child with a red fez as a reminiscence of the original image (fig. 54).[348] With Bonhomme Banania still being the »most famous, and certainly one of the best-known advertisements ever used in France«, the ›grand enfant‹ turning into a real kid could have been reason enough to en-

346 Susan J. Terrio: Crafting the Culture and History of French Chocolate, pp. 250-251.

347 Dana S. Hale: French Images of Race on Product Trademarks during the Third Republic, pp. 144-145.

348 Y'a bon Banania ou Y'a pas bon Banania. Fig. 54: Banania box (2005), ibid.

rage anti-racist activists.[349] Yet, it was Banania's continuous promotion and production of vintage merchandising and traditional editions that resulted in charges being brought against them by organisations such as the *Mouvement contre le Racisme et pour l'Amitié entre les Peuples* (MRAP).[350] On May 19th, 2011, the appellate court of Versailles ordered the proprietors of the company to entirely stop spreading products carrying the slogan ›Y'a bon‹.[351]

Vincent Howell, executive of Mars, Inc., could have acted as a spokesman for all three companies when he justified the ineffectual transformation of Uncle Ben by stating that there was »a timeless element to him, we didn't want to significantly change him«.[352] In strikingly similar patterns, each icon first became hugely popular, was criticised over the course of social movements, was subsequently modified and marginalised, but was eventually revived with a new look, while clearly building on the recognition-value of the original characters. After a period of political correctness, the acceptance of traditional racial stereotypes has, seemingly, increased, although in the meantime racialised advertising has most frequently dealt with issues of multiculturalism or ironically-referenced racist representations.[353] Anne Donadey explains this trend as »a subtle reinforcing of feelings of superiority, in part through the perverse pleasure of viewing non-›PC‹ images in a ›PC‹ era which is experienced as limiting by many members of dominant groups«.[354] Thus, it might actually be the perception of limitation that enabled the relaunch of the written-off racial images in the new millennium, rather than their attempted democratisation. What remains remarkable is the cross-border concurrent timing of the happenings, despite the fact that each country witnessed individual discourses of race in the context of either slavery or colonialism and despite the difference between the initially-contested and later-revived stereotypes.

349 Robert Aldrich: Greater France, p. 259.
350 Sébastien Durand: Storytelling: le ›Y'a bon Banania‹ est-il raciste?.
351 ›Y'a bon Banania‹ disparaîtra bel et bien.
352 Cited in Stuart Elliott: Uncle Ben, Board Chairman.
353 Malte Hinrichsen: Promoting Racism, pp. 265-267.
354 Anne Donadey: ›Y'a bon Banania‹, p. 17.

4. Conclusion

> »I subjected myself to an objective examination, I discovered my blackness, my ethnic characteristics; and I was battered down by tom-toms, cannibalism, intellectual deficiency, fetishism, racial defects, slave-ships, and above all else, above all: ›Sho' good eatin'‹.« (Frantz Fanon)[355]

In the 1960s, when Charles Lam Markmann translated Frantz Fanon's *Peau noire, masques blancs* for an English-speaking audience in America that was witnessing »a time of extraordinary political and social upheaval«, he »completely eradicate[d] Fanon's use of phenomenology, and instead of linking him to Sartre [...] place[d] him in the black/white relationship of the U.S. South«.[356] Despite all philosophical inaccuracy, however, both Richard Philcox and Paul Gilroy identify a slogan of plain material culture – »Sho' good eatin'« – as the most striking example of Markmann's »inappropriately Americanised translation«.[357] Nevertheless, it is short-sighted to interpret this translation of »Y'a bon Banania« as merely a »crude Americanisation of a powerful French-colonial stereotype«.[358] It rather reveals, albeit incidentally, the global scope of Fanon's experience.

Finding the same slogan rendered as »Oh Dem Watermelons« in the English edition of Dany Laferrière's *Comment faire l'amour avec un Nègre sans se fatigue*, Jana Evans Braziel acknowledges both translators' merit of having »capture[d] the racialized parameters of food and eating within the United States«.[359] While lacking the sensitivity to do justice to the singularity of the authors' biographical narratives and the specific connotations of the Banania advertising, Markman and his colleague Homel were, nevertheless, able to realise that blacks in America were subjected to a similar

355 Frantz Fanon: Black Skin White Masks, p. 79.

356 Richard Philcox interviewed by Celia Britton, in Frantz Fanon: Retrieving a Lost Voice, pp. 4-5.

357 Paul Gilroy: Darker than Blue, p. 12.

358 Robbie Shilliam: A Fanonian Critique of Lebow's A Cultural Theory of International Relations, p. 127.

359 Jana Evans Braziel: Artists, Performers, and Black Masculinity in the Haitian Diaspora, p. 48. Dany Laferrière has been translated to English by David Homel in How to Make Love to a Negro.

racism, particularly in commodity culture.[360] With the »language of [...] ads« in America often being »›bastardized‹ black English«, numerous U.S. companies since the late 19th century have relied on racial stereotyping to promote a variety of products and, thus, confronted the black population with »the fact of blackness«, as Fanon (or rather Markmann) put it.[361]

Ever since economic exchanges with Africa increased in late medieval times and the transatlantic slave trade developed during the Renaissance and early modernity, there have been discourses on blacks and blackness which always mirror social and political roles of Africans in new multiethnic societies. Whereas in Europe, the imported servants were a privilege of the elites and evoked memories of blacks in service of Muslim rulers, the U.S. plantation system, from the 17th century onwards, equated Africans with slaves and an institution of slavery that was far from bearing connotations of luxury. When Enlightenment philosophies and rising natural sciences started to provide racialised justifications for the global system of exploitation, these included both dehumanising concepts of blacks as apelike savages, as well as ›positive‹ interpretations of their naturalness as the cradle of a primitive goodness.

In controversies between abolitionists and pro-slavery activists in the United States, both sides propagated the stereotype of the kind-hearted black with the only difference being that the latter interpreted it as a result of the civilising impact of a white slave society. Building on traditional European perceptions of black servants, this image of the contented slave was able to become a global concept with the publication of Harriet Beecher Stowe's *Uncle Tom's Cabin*, which further ridiculed and emasculated blacks through successful minstrel adaptation. In the meantime, the traditional European moor had also absorbed connotations of

360 The parallels are illustrated by Pierre E. Cudmore who calls the »Banania« figure a »French Aunt Jemima« and by Jana Evans Braziel who states that the racialised »Banania« images in France »are as pervasive as ones of Aunt Jemima and Uncle Ben are in the U.S.«. Cf. Pierre E. Cudmore: From Banania to Chocolat, p. 97; Jana E. Braziel: Trans-American Constructions of Black Masculinity, p. 889.

361 Walter M. Brasch: Black English and the Mass Media, p. 114; Frantz Fanon: Black Skin White Masks, p. 77. A more recent assessment of African American English in advertising can be found in Jane H. Hill: The Everyday Language of White Racism, esp. pp. 166-169.

slavish docility and, through constant representation in the service of white mistresses, had become a humiliating stereotype, which, like the American »Sambo« images, formed the antithesis to depictions of savage African warriors fighting colonising troops and raping innocent white women. Consequently, the deriding and harmless representations on both sides of the Atlantic constituted a possibility of overcoming anxieties about racial otherness and, especially in times of social and economic pressure, enabled the ideological inclusion of under-classes, while excluding racialised outsiders.

From the late 19th century onwards, the racial and social hierarchy that was visualised in the images of docile slaves, Oriental servants or, particularly in France, benevolent colonial soldiers became marketable through various commodities. Implicitly referring to the consumption of colonial produce, or other racialised products, as a possible form of harmlessly incorporating the fascination of otherness into daily life, chocolate, coffee, rice and soap were particularly promoted with motifs of race and complexion. Reproducing power structures of past social orders, these advertisements sold feelings of superiority to white consumers and accumulated money for white producers. In accordance with this global pattern, German, French and U.S. companies used specific, convenient images to participate in this form of commodity racism and, with the success of their trademark figures, exemplified the two-faced character of racist ideologies.

Just shortly after the Southern states' lynch justice killed thousands of blacks because they were supposedly threatening white women and while segregation policies still organised the U.S. society along colour lines, Uncle Ben personified the alleged docility of Antebellum domestic slaves in supermarkets across the country. When German intellectuals and media waged a campaign against the occupation of the Rhineland by French colonial soldiers and propaganda spread the word of ›Rassenschande‹ more than a decade before the Nazi-era, the Sarotti-Mohr successfully promoted his exotic and chocolaty services. These attacked troops, in turn, were at the centre of racial discourses in France, but regarded as benevolent children (such as Bonhomme Banania) which only unleash their savage warrior potential against the enemies of the beloved French nation.

Seemingly paradoxical, this duality is, in fact, a central element in processes of othering. Difference has always been the source of both fear and fascination and, in the case of racism, has »been constructed in order to be serviceable to those who are historically dominant«.[362] Thus, when blacks became viewed as representatives of economical and political inferiority over the course of the slave trade, their relatively neutral and marginal image was charged with messages of differentiation and started to occupy a prominent position in European and U.S. American iconography. In this context, the 20th century simultaneity of servant and rapist images, for example, merely continued a tradition of dualistic perceptions with both representations emphasising the difference of the racial others.

In striking parallelism, however, these images of difference were contested in France, Germany and the United States in the decades following the 1960s. Influenced by the racist catastrophe of the Holocaust and building on the struggle of African Americans against Jim Crow legislation, a notion of racial sensitivity and political correctness led to the temporary condemnation of traditional derogatory representations. Public discourses on racial otherness changed, but did not disappear and found new representations applicable in international advertising. Products like Virginia Slims cigarettes and brands such as Benetton focused on motifs of multiculturalism, but in the attempt to create images of race unification ended up reproducing the categorical implications of the concept of race.[363] It would require further studies to identify the reasons for the revival of traditional racial stereotypes in advertising and its effects on consumer behaviour and product sales, but a widespread negative perception of supposedly ›limiting‹ political correctness may have contributed to recent campaigns using racial connotations and to the, again concomitant, reanimations of Uncle Ben, Bonhomme Banania and the Sarotti-Mohr.

In conclusion, the study of trademark stereotypes can shed light on historical conditions and contemporary realities of racial exclusion. It can offer insights into the social psychology of consumption as well as information about the social connotations of food. As early representatives of a transatlantic popular culture, these stereotypes mirror the complex interactions between Amer-

362 Michael Pickering: Stereotyping, p. 75.

363 Cf. Minjeong Kim and Angie Y. Chung: Consuming Orientalism; Henry A. Giroux: Consuming Social Change.

ican and European iconographies and exemplify their development throughout the centuries. Finally, as Fanon's lament vividly demonstrates, they were an important part of blacks' physical experience of white superiority and, thus, affected the self-awareness of those stereotyped in societies of alleged equality and democracy. Due to these potential applications to academic research, the trademark imagery of contented slaves and childlike servants should serve to greatly contribute to the advancement of racism analysis, rather than to continuously ›serve‹ consumers around the world.[364]

364 The finalisation of this book would not have been possible without the support of many people. First I want to express my gratitude to the Department of History of the Universtity of Essex, in particular to Matthias Röhrig Assunçao and Jeremy Krikler, for providing assistance throughout my research in Colchester on which this book is based. The invaluable advice given by Wulf D. Hund and Stefanie Affeldt has been a great help towards the completion of the manuscript. My special thanks go to my friend Elizabeth Barrett for patiently introducing me to some subtleties of the English language. Finally, I wish to thank my parents and Anna to whom this book is dedicated.

5. Bibliography

(Non-English quotations are my translations. Emphases in the originals are not included.)

About Uncle Ben's, http://www.unclebens.com/about.aspx [27.04.2006].

Acker, Alison: Honduras. The Making of a Banana Republic. Toronto: Between the Lines 1988.

Afoakwa, Emmanuel O.: Chocolate Science and Technology. Chichester etc.: John Wiley 2010.

Agnew, Jeremy: Entertainment in the Old West. Theater, Music, Circuses, Medicine Shows, Pricefighting and Other Popular Amusements. Jefferson: McFarland 2011.

Aldrich, Robert: Greater France. A History of French Overseas Expansion. Houndmills etc.: Macmillan 1996.

Allen, Gary J., and Albala, Ken (eds.): The Business of Food. Encyclopedia of the Food and Drink Industries. Westport etc.: Greenwood 2007.

Allport, Gordon W.: The Nature of Prejudice. Reading (Mass.): Addison-Wesley 1954.

Ammons, Elizabeth (ed.): Harriet Beecher Stowe's Uncle Tom's Cabin. A Casebook. Oxford etc.: Oxford University Press 2007.

Amussen, Susan D.: Caribbean Exchanges. Slavery and the Transformation of English Society, 1640-1700. Chapel Hill: University of North Carolina Press 2007.

Anderson, Benedict: Imagined Communities. Reflections on the Origin and the Spread of Nationalism. Rev. and ext. ed. London etc.: Verso 1991.

Andrees, Dirks: Der Sarotti-Mohr – oder die Geschichte einer ewig jungen Werbefigur. In: Im deutschen Reich der Zwerge, Riesen und Schutzengel. Mythen von Kirche und Kapital, ed. by Friedrich Knilli et al. München: Hanser 1974, pp. 132-139.

Archer Straw, Petrine: Negrophilia. Avant-garde Paris and Black Culture in the 1920s. London: Thames & Hudson 2000.

Armitage, David, and Subrahmanyam, Sanjay (eds.): The Age of Revolutions in Global Context, c. 1760-1840. Basingstoke: Palgrave Macmillan 2010.

Auslander, Leora, and Holt, Thomas C.: Sambo in Paris. Race and Racism in the Iconography of the Everyday. In: The Color of Liberty. Histories of Race in France, ed. by Sue Peabody, Tyler Stovall. Durham etc.: Duke University Press 2003, pp. 147-184.

Bachollet, Raymond et al.: Négripub. L'image des Noirs dans la publicité. Paris: Somogy 1992.

Badenberg, Nana: Mohrenwäschen, Völkerschauen. Der Konsum des Schwarzen um 1900. In: Colors 1800/1900/2000: Signs of Ethnic

Difference, ed. by Birgit Tautz. Amsterdam: Rodopi 2004, pp. 163-184.

Baker, Stacey M., Motley, Carol M., and Henderson, Geraldine R.: From Despicable to Collectible. The Evolution of Collective Memories for and the Value of Black Advertising Memorabilia. In: Journal of Advertising, 33, 2004, 3, pp. 37-50.

Baldwin, Brooke: The Cakewalk. A Study in Stereotype and Reality. In: Journal of Social History, 15, 1981, 2, pp. 205-218.

Baldwin, James: Everybody's Protest Novel. In: id., Notes of a Native Son. London: Joseph 1964, pp. 19-28.

—: Many Thousands Gone. In: id., Notes of a Native Son. London: Joseph 1964, pp. 29-47.

Balibar, Etienne, and Wallerstein, Immanuel: Race, Nation, Class. Ambiguous Identities. London etc.: Routledge 1988.

Bancel, Nicolas, and Blanchard, Pascal: Civiliser. L'invention de L'indigène. In: Culture Coloniale. La France conquise par son empire, 1871-1931, ed. by Pascal Blanchard and Sandrine Lemaire. Paris: Autrement 2003, pp. 149-161.

Barker, David: Identity and Psychopathology. In: Main Issues in Mental Health and Race, ed. by David Ndegwa and Dele Olajide. Aldershot etc.: Ashgate 2003, pp. 65-87.

Barnes, Michael S.: The Tom Caricature. In: Authentic History Center, 2012, http://www.authentichistory.com/diversity/african/2-tom/index.html [10.09.2012].

Baudrillard, Jean: The System of Objects, transl. by James Benedict. London etc.: Verso 1996.

Bendix, Regina: Of ›Mohrenköpfe‹ and ›Japanesen‹. Swiss Images of the Foreign. In: Journal of Folklore Research, 30, 1993, 1, pp. 15-28.

Benedict, Burton: The Anthropology of World's Fairs. San Francisco's Panama Pacific International Exposition of 1915. London etc.: Scolar 1983.

Benjamin, Walter: The Arcades Project, transl. by Howard Eiland and Kevin McLaughlin. Cambridge (Mass.) etc.: Harvard University Press 1999.

Bergsma, John S., and Hahn, Scott W.: Noah's Nakedness and the Curse on Canaan (Genesis 9:20-27). In: Journal of Biblical Literature, 124, 2005, 1, pp. 25-40.

Berlin, Ira, and Hoffman, Ronald (eds.): Slavery and Freedom in the Age of the American Revolution. Charlottesville: University Press of Virginia 1983.

—: Many Thousands Gone. The First Two Centuries of Slavery in North America. Cambridge (Mass.) etc.: Belknap Press of Harvard University Press 1998.

Berliner, Brett A.: Ambivalent Desire. The Exotic Black Other in Jazz-

Age France. Amherst etc.: University of Massachusetts Press 2002.

Bernasconi, Robert: Kant as an Unfamiliar Source of Racism. In: Philosophers on Race. Critical Essays, ed. by Julie K. Ward and Tommy L. Lott. Oxford etc.: Blackwell 2002, pp. 145-166.

Beriss, David: Culture-as-Race or Culture-as-Culture. In: Race in France. Interdisciplinary Perspectives on the Politics of Difference, ed. by Herrick Chapman and Laura L. Frader. New York etc.: Berghahn 2004, pp. 111-140.

Berry, Christopher J.: The Social Theory of the Scottish Enlightenment. Edinburgh: Edinburgh University Press 1997.

Bestor, Jane F.: Titian's portrait of Laura Eustochia. The decorum of female beauty and the motif of the black page. In: Renaissance Studies, 17, 2003, 4, pp. 628-673.

Blackburn, Robin: The Making of New World Slavery. From the Baroque to the Modern, 1492-1800. London: Verso 2010.

Blakely, Allison: Blacks in the Dutch World. The Evolution of Racial Imagery in a Modern Society. Bloomington etc.: Indiana University Press 1993.

Blanchard, Pascal, and Chatelier, Armelle (eds.): Images et Colonies. Nature, discours et influence de l'iconographie coloniale liée à la propagande coloniale et à la représentation des Africains et de l'Afrique en France, de 1920 aux Indépendances. Paris: Syros 1993.

Blanks, David R., and Frassetto, Michael (eds.): Western Views of Islam in Medieval and Early Modern Europe. New York: St. Martin's Press 1999.

—: Western Views of Islam in the Premodern Period. A Brief History of Past Approaches. In: Western Views of Islam in Medieval and Early Modern Europe, ed. by David R. Blanks and Michael Frassetto. New York: St. Martin's Press 1999, pp. 11- 53.

Blassingame, John W.: The Slave Community. Plantation Life in the Antebellum South. Oxford: Oxford University Press 1972.

Bloom, John: Cardboard Patriarchy. Adult Baseball Card Collecting and the Nostalgia for a Presexual Past. In: Hop on Pop. The Politics and Pleasures of Popular Culture, ed. by Henry Jenkins et al.. Durham: Duke University Press 2002, pp. 66-87.

Bloom, Peter: French Colonial Documentary. Mythologies of Humanitarianism. Minneapolis etc.: University of Minnesota Press 2008.

Bobb, Vilna B.: Neither Ignorance nor Bliss. Race, Racism, and the West Indian Immigrant Experience. In: Migration, Transnationalization, and Race in a Changing New York, ed. by Héctor R. Cordero-Guzmán, Robert C. Smith and Ramón Grosfuguel. Philadelphia: Temple University Press 2001, pp. 212-238.

Bogle, Donald: Toms, Coons, Mulattoes, Mammies & Bucks. An Interpretive History of Blacks in American Films, 3rd ed. Oxford: Round-

house 1994.
Bonnett, Alastair: How the British Working Class Became White. The Symbolic (Re)formation of Racialized Capitalism. In: Journal of Historical Sociology, 11, 1998, 3, pp. 316-340.
—: Anti-Racism. London etc.: Routledge 2000.
Boskin, Joseph: Sambo. The Rise & Demise of an American Jester. New York etc.: Oxford University Press 1986.
Bräunlein, Peter J.: Von Mohren-Apotheken und Mohrenkopf-Wappen. In:Zeitschrift für Kulturaustausch, 41, 1991, 2, pp. 219-238.
Brasch, Walter M.: Black English and the Mass Media. Amherst: University of Massachusetts Press 1981.
Bratton, Jacqueline S.: English Ethiopians. British Audiences and Black-Face Acts, 1835-1865. In: The Yearbook of English Studies, 11, 1981, pp. 127-142.
Braziel, Jana E.: Trans-American Constructions of Black Masculinity. Dany Laferrière, le Nègre, and the Late Capitalist American Racial machine-désirante. In: Callaloo, 26, 2003, 3, pp. 867-900.
—: Artists, Performers, and Black Masculinity in the Haitian Diaspora. Bloomington: Indiana University Press 2008.
Breckenridge, Carol A.: The Aesthetics and Politics of Colonial Collecting. India at World Fairs. In: Comparative Studies in Society and History, 31, 1989, 2, pp. 195-216.
Bristor, Julia M., Lee, Renée G., and Hunt, Michelle R.: Race and Ideology. African-American Images in Television Advertising. In: Journal of Public Policy & Marketing, 14, 1995, 1, pp. 48-59.
Brown, Bill: Reification, Reanimation, and the American Uncanny. In: Critical Inquiry, 32, 2006, 2, pp. 175-207.
Brown, Elspeth H.: Black models and the Invention of the US ›Negro Market‹, 1945-1960. In: Inside Marketing. Practices, Ideologies, Devices, ed. by Detlev Zwick and Julien Cayla. Oxford etc.: Oxford University Press 2011, pp. 185-211.
Brown, Nikki L. M., and Stentiford, Barry M. (eds.): The Jim Crow Encyclopedia, Vol. 1, 2. Westport: Greenwood 2008.
Brumfitt, Keith, et al. (eds.): Vocational Business, Vol. 2: The Competitive Business Environment. Cheltenham: Nelson Thornes 2001.
Bucheli, Marcelo: Bananas and Business. The United Fruit Company in Colombia, 1899-2000. New York etc.: New York University Press 2005.
Burke, Peter: Eyewitnessing. The Uses of Images as Historical Evidence. London: Reaktion 2001.
Carney, Judith A.: Black Rice. The African Origins of Rice Cultivation in the Americas. Cambridge (Mass.) etc.: Harvard University Press 2001.
—: The African Antecedents of Uncle Ben in U.S. Rice History. In: Jour-

nal of Historical Geography, 29, 2003, 1, pp. 1-21.
—: ›With Grains in Her Hair‹. Rice in Colonial Brazil. In: Slavery & Abolition, 25, 2004, 1, pp. 1-27.
Carroll, Anne E.: Word, Image, and the New Negro. Representation and Identity in the Harlem Renaissance. Bloomington etc.: Indiana University Press 2007.
Casmier-Paz, Lynn: Heritage, not Hate? Collecting Black Memorabilia. In: Southern Cultures, 9, 2003, 1, pp. 43-61.
Castro, Daniel: Another Face of Empire. Bartholomé de las Casas, Indigenous Rights, and Ecclesiastical Imperialism. Durham etc.: Duke University Press 2007.
Cateau, Heather, and Carrington, Selwyn H. H. (eds.): Capitalism and Slavery Fifty Years Later. Eric Eustace Williams – A Reassessment of the Man and His Work. New York: Peter Lang 2000.
Chalaye, Sylvie: Du Noir au nègre. L'image du Noir au théâtre (1550-1960). Paris: Harmattan 1998.
Chaney, Michael A.: Fugitive Vision. Slave Image and Black Identity in Antebellum Narrative. Bloomington: Indiana University Press 2008.
Chapman, Peter: Bananas. How the United Fruit Company Shaped the World. Edinburgh etc.: Canongate 2007.
Chase, David (prod.): Proshai, Livushka. In: The Sopranos, season 3, episode 2 (original air date 4 March 2001).
Ciarlo, David: Advertising and the Optics of Colonial Power at the Fin de Siècle. In: German Colonialism, Visual Culture, and Modern Memory, ed. by Volker M. Langbehn. New York etc.: Routledge 2010, pp. 37-54.
—: Advertising Empire. Race and Visual Culture in Imperial Germany. Cambridge (Mass.) etc.: Harvard University Press 2011.
Clark, Andrew: Uncle Ben promoted to the board. In: Guardian, 30 March 2007, http://www.guardian.co.uk/media/2007/mar/30/marketingandpr.race [10.09.2011].
Cockrell, Dale: Demons of Disorder. Early Blackface Minstrels and Their World. Cambridge etc.: Cambridge University Press 1997.
Coe, Sophie D., and Coe, Michael D.: The True History of Chocolate. London: Simon & Schuster 1996.
Colby, Jason M.: ›Banana Growing and Negro Management‹. Race, Labor, and Jim Crow Colonialism in Guatemala, 1884-1930. In: Diplomatic History, 30, 2006, 4, pp. 595-621.
Conley, Tom: Identity. Never More. In: Identity Papers. Contested Nationhood in Twentieth-Century France, ed. by Steven Ungar and Tom Conley. Minneapolis: University of Minnesota Press 1996, pp. 272-282.
Cornils, Ingo: Denkmalsturz. The German Student Movement and German Colonialism. In: German Colonialism and National Identity, ed.

by Michael Perraudin and Jürgen Zimmerer. New York etc.: Routledge 2011, pp. 197-212.
Cortese, Anthony J.: Provocateur. Images of Women and Minorities in Advertising. Lanham etc.: Rowman & Littlefield 2008.
Cserno, Isabell: Pancakes, Chocolate, and the Trap of Eternal Servitude. A Reading of Race in the United States and Germany. In: Color, Hair, and Bone. Race in the Twenty-first Century, ed. by Linden Lewis and Glyne Griffith. Lewisburg: Bucknell University Press 2008, pp. 69-101.
—: Race and Mass Consumption in Consumer Culture. National Trademark Advertising in the United States and Germany, 1890-1930. Unpublished doctoral thesis (College Park, 2008).
Cudmore, Pierre E.: From Banania to Chocolat. The French Colonization of Africa and Contemporary Cinema. In: Atenea, 15, 1995, 1-2, pp. 95-103.
Dabydeen, David: Hogarth's Blacks. Images of Blacks in Eighteenth Century English Art. Mundelstrup etc.: Dangaroo 1985.
Davis, David B.: The Problem of Slavery in Western Culture. Ithaca: Cornell University Press 1966.
—: Inhuman Bondage. The Rise and Fall of Slavery in the New World. Oxford etc.: Oxford University Press 2006.
Deaville, James: Cakewalk in Waltz Time? African-American Music in Jahrhundertwende Vienna. In: Reverberations. Representations of Modernity, Tradition and Cultural Value in/between Central Europe and North America, ed. by Susan Ingram et al. Frankfurt a. M. etc.: Peter Lang 2002, pp. 17-39.
Debost, Jean-Barthélemi: La publicité lave plus blanc. In: Images et Colonies. Nature, discours et influence de l'iconographie coloniale liée à la propagande coloniale et à la représentation des Africains et de l'Afrique en France, de 1920 aux Indépendances, ed. by Pascal Blanchard and Armelle Chatelier. Paris: Syros 1993, pp. 97-102.
Demel, Walter: Wie die Chinesen gelb wurden. Ein Beitrag zur Frühgeschichte der Rassentheorien. In: Historische Zeitschrift, 255, 1992, 3, pp. 625-666.
Dixon, Thomas: The Clansman. London: William Heinemann 1905.
Djaït, Hichem: Europe and Islam, 1st eng. ed., transl. by Peter Heinegg. Berkeley etc.: University of California Press 1985.
Dobie, Madeleine: Trading Places. Colonization and Slavery in Eighteenth-Century French Culture. Ithaca: Cornell University Press 2010.
Donadey, Anne: ›Y'a bon Banania‹. Ethics and Cultural Criticism in the Colonial Context. In: French Cultural Studies, 11, 2000, pp. 9-29.
Dreesbach, Anne: Gezähmte Wilde. Die Zurschaustellung ›exotischer‹ Menschen in Deutschland 1870-1940. Frankfurt a. M.: Campus 2005.
Dubin, Steven C.: Symbolic Slavery. Black Representations in Popular

Culture. In: Social Problems, 34, 1987, 2, pp. 122-140.

Du Bois, W. E. B.: The Souls of White Folk (1st ed.: New York, 1920), republished in Du Bois: Writings. New York etc.: Literary Classics of the United States 1986, pp. 923-938.

Dunson, Stephanie: Black Misrepresentation in Nineteenth-Century Sheet Music Illustration. In: Beyond Blackface. African Americans and the Creation of American Popular Culture, 1890-1930, ed. by W. Fitzhugh Brundage. Chapel Hill etc.: University of North Carolina Press 2011, pp. 45-65.

Durand, Sébastien: Storytelling. le ›Y'a bon Banania‹ est-il raciste?. In: Le Post, 23 January 2009, http://www.lepost.fr/article/2009/01/23/1 3 98118_storytelling-le-y-a-bon-banania-est-il-raciste.html [10.09.2011].

Echenberg, Myron: Colonial Conscripts. The Tirailleurs Sénégalais in French West Africa, 1857-1960. Portsmouth etc.: James Currey 1991.

Elkins, Stanley M.: Slavery. A Problem in American Institutional and Intellectual Life. Chicago etc.: University of Chicago Press 1959.

Ellingson, Ter: The Myth of the Noble Savage. Berkely etc.: University of California Press 2001.

Elliott, Stuart: Uncle Ben, Board Chairman. In: The New York Times, 30 March 2007, http://www.nytimes.com/2007/03/30/business/me dia/30adco.html [10.09.2011].

Ellison, Ralph: Invisible Man, 1952, 2nd ed. New York etc.: Vintage 1995).

Eltis, David: The Rise of African Slavery in the Americas. Cambridge etc.: Cambridge University Press 2000.

—, Morgan, Philip, and Richardson, David: Agency and Diaspora in Atlantic History. Reassessing the African Contribution to Rice Cultivation in the Americas. In: American Historical Review, 112, 2007, 5, pp. 1329-1358.

Erickson, Jon: The Face and the Possibility of an Ethics of Performance. In: Journal of Dramatic Theory and Criticism, 13, 1999, 2, pp. 5-22.

Euraque, Darío A.: The Threat of Blackness to the Mestizo Nation. Race and Ethnicity in the Honduran Banana Economy, 1920s and 1930s. In: Banana Wars. Power, Production, and History in the Americas, ed. by Steve Striffler and Mark Moberg. Durham: Duke University Press 2003, pp. 229-250.

Fanon, Frantz: Peau noire, masques blancs. Paris: Editions du Seuil 1952.

—: Black Skin, White Masks, 1st eng. ed., transl. by Charles L. Markmann. London: MacGibbon & Kee 1968.

Fehrenbach, Heide: Afro-German Children and the Social Politics of Race after 1945. In: German History from the Margins, ed. by Neil Gregor, Nils Roemer and Mark Roseman. Bloomington: Indiana University Press 2006, pp. 226-251.

—: Black Occupation Children and the Devolution of the Nazi Racial State. In: After the Nazi Racial State. Difference and Democracy in Germany and Europe, ed. by Rita Chin et al. Ann Arbor: University of Michigan Press 2009, pp. 30-54.

Fiedler, Matthias: Zwischen Abenteuer, Wissenschaft und Kolonialismus. Der deutsche Afrikadiskurs im 18. Und 19. Jahrhundert. Köln: Böhlau 2005.

Fields-Black, Edda L.: Deep Roots. Rice Farmers in West Africa and the African Diaspora. Bloomington: Indiana University Press 2008.

Fock, Stefanie: ›Un individu de raça negroide‹. El Negro und die Wunderkammern des Rassismus. In: Entfremdete Körper. Rassismus als Leichenschändung, ed. by Wulf D. Hund. Bielefeld: Transcript 2009, pp. 165-204.

Fredrickson, George M.: The Black Image in the White Mind. The Debate on Afro-American Character and Destiny, 1817-1914. New York: Harper & Row 1971.

—: The Arrogance of Race. Historical Perspectives on Slavery, Racism, and Social Inequality. Middletown: Wesleyan University Press 1988.

Frow, John: Time and Commodity Culture. Essays on Cultural Theory and Postmodernity. Oxford: Oxford University Press 1997.

Garrett, Debbie B.: Black Dolls. A Comprehensive Guide to Celebrating, Collecting, and Experiencing the Passion. Dallas: self-published 2008.

Garrigues, Jean: Banania. Histoire d'une Passion Française. Paris: Du May 1991.

Gates, Henry L. (ed.): The Annotated Uncle Tom's Cabin. New York etc.: W. W. Norton 2007.

Gaskell, Ivan: History of Images. In: New Perspectives on Historical Writing, ed. by Peter Burke. Cambridge: Polity Press 1991, pp. 168-192.

Genovese, Eugene D.: Rebelliousness and Docility in the Negro Slave. A Critique of the Elkins Thesis. In: The Debate Over Slavery. Stanley Elkins and His Critics, ed. by Ann J. Lane. Urbana: University of Illinois Press 1971, pp. 43-74.

—: Roll, Jordan, Roll. The World the Slaves Made. (New York etc.: Pantheon 1974.

Gilroy, Paul: Darker than Blue. On the Moral Economies of Black Atlantic Culture. Cambridge (Mass.) etc.: Belknap Press of Harvard University Press 2010.

Giroux, Henry A.: Consuming Social Change. The ›United Colors of Benetton‹. In: Cultural Critique, 26, 1993, pp. 5-32.

Gissis, Snait B.: Visualizing ›Race‹ in the Eighteenth Century. In: Historical Studies in the Natural Sciences, 41, 2011, 1, pp. 41-103.

Glickman, Lawrence B.: ›Buy for the Sake of the Slave‹. Abolition-

ism and the Origins of American Consumer Activism. In: American Quarterly, 56, 2004, 4, pp. 889-912.
Goings, Kenneth W.: Mammy and Uncle Mose. Black Collectibles and American Stereotyping. Bloomington: Indiana University Press 1994.
Goldberg, David T.: Liberalism's Limits. Carlyle and Mill on ›The Negro Question‹. In: Philosophers on Race. Critical Essays, ed. by Julie K. Ward and Tommy L. Lott. Oxford etc.: Blackwell 2002, pp. 195-204.
Goldenberg, David M.: The Curse of Ham. Race and Slavery in Early Judaism, Christianity, and Islam. Princeton etc.: Princeton University Press 2003.
Gordon, Bertram M.: Chocolate in France. Evolution of a Luxury Product. In: Chocolate. History, Culture, and Heritage, ed. by Louis E. Grivetti and Howard-Yana Shapiro. Hoboken: Wiley 2009, pp. 569-582.
Greene, Larry A.: Race in the Reich. The African American Press on Nazi Germany. In: Germans and African Americans. Two Centuries of Exchange, ed. by Larry A. Greene and Anke Ortlepp. Jackson: University Press of Mississippi 2011, pp. 70-87.
Griffith, David W. (dir.): The Birth of a Nation, 1915.
Gudermann, Rita: Der Sarotti-Mohr. Die bewegte Geschichte einer Werbefigur. Berlin: Ch. Links 2004.
Gutman, Herbert G.: The Black Family in Slavery and Freedom, 1750-1925. Oxford: Blackwell 1976.
Hahn, Thomas: The Difference the Middle Ages Makes. Color and Race before the Modern World. In: Journal of Medieval and Early Modern Studies, 31, 2001, 1, pp. 1-37.
Hale, Dana S.: French Images of Race on Product Trademarks during the Third Republic. In: The Color of Liberty. Histories of Race in France, ed. by Sue Peabody and Tyler Stovall. Durham etc.: Duke University Press 2003, pp. 131-146.
—: Races on Display. French Representations of Colonized Peoples, 1886-1940. Bloomington etc.: Indiana University Press 2008.
Hale, Grace E.: *Making Whiteness. The Culture of Segregation in the South, 1890-1940.* New York etc.: Vintage 1998.
Hall, John R., Neitz, Mary J., and Battani, Marshall: *Sociology on Culture.* New York: Routledge 2003.
Hall, Stuart (ed.): Representation. Cultural Representations and Signifying Practices. London etc.: Sage 1997.
—: The Spectacle of the ›Other‹. In: Representation. Cultural Representations and Signifying Practices, ed. by Stuart Hall. London etc.: Sage 1997, pp. 223-290.
Hardin, Marie: Argument: Stereotypes are the best way to give consumers a quick understanding of the creative impact of the message. In:

Advertising and Society. Controversies and Consequences, ed. by Carol J. Pardun. Malden: Wiley-Blackwell 2009, pp. 130-135.

Harris, Michael D.: Colored Pictures. Race and Visual Representation. Chapel Hill etc.: University of North Carolina Press 2003.

Hattersheimer Geschichtsverein 1985 e. V. (ed.): Machbarkeitsstudie. Ein Museum für Hattersheim am Main, 2007. In: http://www.geschichtsverein-hattersheim.de/uploads/ media/Expertise.pdf [27.08.2011].

Haug, Wolfgang F.: Critique of Commodity Aesthetics. Appearance, Sexuality and Advertising in Capitalist Society (1st ed. 1971), transl. by Robert Bock. Cambridge etc.: Polity Press 1986.

Hawthorne, Walter: From Africa to Brazil. Culture, Identity, and an Atlantic Slave Trade, 1630-1830. Cambridge etc.: Cambridge University Press 2010.

Haynes, Stephen R.: Noah's Curse. The Biblical Justification of American Slavery. Oxford etc.: Oxford University Press 2002.

Herder, Johann G.: Briefe zur Beförderung der Humanität (1st ed. 1797). In: id., Sämtliche Werke, Vol. 18, ed. by Bernhard Suphan. Hildesheim etc.: Olms 1883.

Hess, Jonathan M.: Germans, Jews and the Claim of Modernity. New Haven etc.: Yale University Press 2002.

Hickethier, Knut: Wundertüten, Überraschungseier, Sammelbilder. Medienverbund in der kommerziellen Kinderkultur In: Ästhetik und Kommunikation, 27, 1977, pp. 28-34.

Hildebrand, Jennifer: Uncovering the True Relationship between Masters and Slaves. In: African Americans in the Nineteenth Century. People and Perspectives, ed. by Dixie R. Haggard. Santa Barbara: ABC-CLIO 2010, pp. 63-78.

Hill, Jane H.: The Everyday Language of White Racism. Chichester etc.: Wiley-Blackwell 2008.

Hinrichsen, Malte: Promoting Racism. Elements of Trademark Stereotyping. In: Racism and Modernity, ed. by Sabine Ritter and Iris Wigger. Berlin etc.: Lit 2011.

Höfert, Almut: Den Feind beschreiben. »Türkengefahr« und europäisches Wissen über das Osmanische Reich 1450-1600. Frankfurt a. M.: Campus 2003.

Hooks, Bell: Black Looks. Race and Representation. Boston: South End Press 1992.

Hornback, Robert: Blackfaced Fools, Black-Headed Birds, Fool Synonyms, and Shakespearean Allusions to Renaissance Blackface Folly. In: Notes and Queries, 55, 2008, 2, pp. 215-219.

Horowitz, Daniel: The Anxieties of Affluence. Critiques of American Consumer Culture, 1939-1979. Amherst: University of Massachusetts Press 2004.

Hudson-Roberts, Wale: Levelling the Field. In: Third Way, 26, 2003, 1,

pp. 9-10.
Hughes, Geoffrey: Political Correctness. A History of Semantics and Culture. Chichester etc.: Wiley-Blackwell 2010.
Hund, Wulf D.: Rassismus. Die soziale Konstruktion natürlicher Ungleichheit. Münster: Westfälisches Dampfboot 1999.
—: Bikini – Die unglücklichen Inseln. In: Blätter für deutsche und internationale Politik, 51, 2006, 7, pp. 870-878.
—: Rassismus. Bielefeld: Transcript 2007.
—: Die weiße Norm. Grundlagen des Farbrassismus. In: Cuerpos Anómalos, ed. by Max S. Hering Torres. Bogotá: Universidad Nacional de Colombia 2008, pp. 171-203.
—: Die Körper der Bilder der Rassen. Wissenschaftliche Leichenschändung und rassistische Entfremdung. In: Entfremdete Körper. Rassismus als Leichenschändung, ed. by Wulf D. Hund. Bielefeld: Transcript 2009, pp. 13-79.
—: Negative Societalisation. Racism and the Constitution of Race. In: Wages of Whiteness & Racist Symbolic Capital, ed. by Wulf D. Hund, Jeremy Krikler and David R. Roediger. Berlin etc.: Lit 2010, pp. 57-96.
Hunwick, John, and Powell, Eve T.: The African Diaspora in the Mediterranean Lands of Islam. Princeton: Markus Wiener 2002.
Husfloen, Kyle (ed.): Black Americana Price Guide. A comprehensive, illustrated guide to African-American collectibles of the 19th & 20th centuries. Dubuque: Antique Trader Books 1996.
Ignatiev, Noel: How the Irish Became White. New York etc.: Routledge 1995.
Ilgen, Volker, and Schindelbeck, Dirk: Jagd auf den Sarotti-Mohr. Von der Leidenschaft des Sammelns. Frankfurt a. M.: Fischer 1997).
Isaac, Benjamin: The Invention of Racism in Classical Antiquity. Princeton etc.: Princeton University Press 2004.
Jahoda, Gustav: Images of Savages. Ancient Roots of Modern Prejudice in Western Culture. London etc.: Routledge 1999.
James, A. Everette: Images of African Americans in Southern Painting, 1840-1940. In: Southern Cultures, 9, 2003, 2, pp. 67-81.
James, C. L. R.: The Black Jacobins. Toussaint L'Ouverture and the San Domingo Revolution. London: Secker & Warburg 1938.
Jefferson, Thomas: Notes on the State of Virginia (1st ed. 1787). In: id., Writings, ed. by Merrill D. Peterson. New York etc.: Library of America 1984), pp. 123-326.
Jordan, Don, and Walsh, Michael: White Cargo. The Forgotten History of Britain's White Slaves in America. New York: New York University Press 2007.
Jordan, Winthrop D.: White Over Black. American Attitudes Toward the Negro, 1550-1812. Chapel Hill: University of North Carolina Press

1968.
Jorgensen, Janice (ed.): Encyclopedia of Consumer Brands. Vol. 1: Consumable Products. Detroit etc.: St. James 1994.
Julien, Pierre: Banania. Legend et réalité. In: Revue d'histoire de la pharmacie, 294, 1992, pp. 275-277.
Jung, Dorothea: Politische Literatur. Rita Gudermann und Bernhard Wulff: ›Der Sarotti-Mohr‹. Die bewegte Geschichte einer Werbefigur. In: Deutschlandfunk (original air date 18 October 2004), http://www.dradio.de/dlf/sendungen/politischeliteratur/316528/ [10.11.2011].
Kaiser, Wolfram: The Great Derby Race. Strategies of Cultural Representation at Nineteenth-Century World Exhibitions. In: Culture and International History, ed. by Jessica C. E. Gienow-Hecht and Frank Schumacher. New York etc.: Berghahn 2004, pp. 45-59.
Kaplan, Paul H. D.: Titian's Laura Dianti and the Origins of the Motif of the Black Page in Portraiture. In: Antichità Viva, 21, 1982, 4, pp. 10-18.
—: Black Africans in Hohenstaufen Iconography. In: Gesta, 26, 1987, 1, pp. 29-36.
Kassarjian, Harold H.: The Negro and American Advertising, 1946-1965. In: Journal of Marketing Research, 6, 1969, 1, pp. 29-39.
Kear, Jon: Vénus noire. Josephine Baker and the Parisian Music-hall. In: Parisian Fields, ed. by Michael Sheringham. London: Reaktion 1996, pp. 46-70.
Kennedy, Deseriee A.: Marketing Goods, Marketing Images. The Impact of Advertising on Race. In: Arizona State Law Journal, 32, 2000, 2, pp. 615-694.
Kern-Foxworth, Marilyn: Aunt Jemima, Uncle Ben, and Rastus. Blacks in Advertising, Yesterday, Today, and Tomorrow. Westport etc.: Greenwood 1994.
Kestling, Robert W.: Blacks under the Swastika: A Research Note. In: The Journal of Negro History, 83, 1998, 1, pp. 84-99.
Kim, Minjeong, and Chung, Angie Y.: Consuming Orientalism. Images of Asian/American Women in Multicultural Advertising. In: Qualitative Sociology, 28, 2005, 1, pp. 67-91.
King, C. Richard: Commodity Racism Now. In: Studies in Symbolic Interaction, Vol. 33, ed. by Norman K. Denzin. Bingley: Emerald 2009, pp. 98-108.
King, C. Richard: Unsettling Commodity Racism. In: Studies in Symbolic Interaction, Vol. 33, ed. by Norman K. Denzin. Bingley: Emerald 2009, pp. 255-273.
Kleber, Thomas: Der Sarotti-Mohr. Zum ikonographischen und literarischen Umfeld einer Werbefigur. Unpublished doctoral thesis, Siegen: 2001.
Koeppel, Dan: Banana. The Fate of the Fruit that Changed the World.

New York: Hudson Street Press 2008.

Koerner, Joseph L.: The Epiphany of the Black Magus circa 1500. In: The Image of the Black in Western Art. Vol. 3, Part 1, ed. by David Bindman and Henry L. Gates, Jr.. Cambridge etc.: Belknap Press of Harvard University Press 2010, pp. 7-92.

Koller, Christian: Der ›Dunkle Verrat an Europa‹. Afrikanische Soldaten im Krieg 1914-1918 in der deutschen Wahrnehmung. In: Zwischen Charleston und Stechschritt. Schwarze im Nationalsozialismus, ed. by Peter Martin and Christine Alonzo. Hamburg etc.: Dölling und Galitz 2004, pp. 111-115.

Kovel, Joel: White Racism. A Psychohistory. New York: Pantheon 1970.

Kruger, Loren: »White Cities,« »Diamond Zulus,« and the »African Contribution to Human Advancement«. African Modernities and the World's Fairs. In: The Drama Review, 51, 2007, 3, pp. 19-45.

Kusser, Astrid: Cakewalking the Anarchy of Empire around 1900. In: German Colonialism, Visual Culture, and Modern Memory, ed. by Volker M. Langbehn. New York etc.: Routledge 2010, pp. 87-104.

Lacey, Barbara E.: Visual Images of Blacks in Early American Imprints. In: The William and Mary Quarterly, 53, 1996, 1, pp. 137-180.

Laferrière, Dany: How to Make Love to a Negro, 1st eng. ed., transl. by David Homel. Toronto: Coach House 1987.

Lane, Ann J. (ed.): The Debate Over Slavery. Stanley Elkins and His Critics. Urbana: University of Illinois Press 1971.

Lane, Barbara G.: Hans Memling. Master Painter in Fifteenth-Century Bruges. London etc.: Harvey Miller 2009.

Langbehn, Volker M. (ed.). German Colonialism, Visual Culture, and Modern Memory. New York etc.: Routledge 2010.

Langley, Lester D.: The Banana Wars. United States Intervention in the Caribbean, 1898-1934. Lexington: University Press of Kentucky 1983.

Lears, Jackson: Fables of Abundance. A Cultural History of Advertising in America. New York: HarperCollins 1994.

Leiter, Andrew B.: In the Shadow of the Black Beast. African American Masculinity in the Harlem and Southern Renaissance. Baton Rouge: Louisiana State University Press 2010.

Lewerenz, Susann: ›Loyal Askari‹ and ›Black Rapist‹. Two Images in the German Discourse on National Identity and Their Impact on the Lives of Black People in Germany, 1918-45. In: German Colonialism and National Identity, ed. by Michael Perraudin and Jürgen Zimmerer. New York etc.: Routledge 2011, pp. 173-183.

Lewis, Bernard: Race and Slavery in the Middle East: An Historical Enquiry. Oxford etc.: Oxford University Press 1990.

Lidchi, Henrietta: The Poetics and the Politics of Exhibiting Other Cultures. In: Representation. Cultural Representations and Signifying

Practices, ed. by Stuart Hall. London etc.: Sage 1997, pp. 151-222.
Lindner, Christoph: Fictions of Commodity Culture. From the Victorian to the Postmodern. Aldershot etc.: Ashgate 2003.
Linné, Carl von: The God-given Order of Nature (extract from The System of Nature, 1735). In: Race and Enlightenment. A Reader, ed. by Emmanuel C. Eze. Cambridge (Mass.) etc.: Blackwell 1997, pp. 10-13.
Littlefield, Daniel C.: Rice and Slaves. Ethnicity and the Slave Trade in Colonial South Carolina. Baton Rouge etc.: Louisiana State University Press 1981.
Lloyd, Catherine: Discourses of Antiracism in France. Aldershot etc.: Ashgate 1998.
Long, Edward: The History of Jamaica, or General Survey of the Antient and Modern State of that Island. 3 Vols. London: T. Lowndes 1774.
Lott, Eric: Love & Theft. Blackface Minstrelsy and the American Working Class. Oxford etc.: Oxford University Press 1995.
Lotz, Rainer E.: Black People. Entertainers of African Descent in Europe and Germany. Bonn: Birgit Lotz 1997.
Lowe, Kate J. P.: The stereotyping of black Africans in Renaissance Europe. In: Black Africans in Renaissance Europe, ed. by Thomas F. Earle and Kate J. P. Lowe, Cambridge etc.: Cambridge University Press 2005, pp. 17-47.
Lunn, Joe: Memoirs of the Maelstrom. A Senegalese Oral History of the First World War. Portsmouth etc.: Heinemann 1999.
Lury, Celia: Consumer Culture, 2nd ed. Cambridge etc.: Polity Press 2011.
Lusane, Clarence: Hitler's Black Victims. The Historical Experiences of Afro-Germans, European Blacks, Africans, and African Americans in the Nazi Era. New York etc.: Routledge 2003.
Macco, Hans: Die Entstehungsgeschichte der Schokoladenfabrik Sarotti. Manuskript im Auftrag von Nestlé verfasst. Berlin: 1931.
—: Rasseprobleme im Dritten Reich. Berlin: P. Schmidt 1933.
MacKenzie, John M. (ed.): Imperialism and Popular Culture. Manchester etc.: Manchester University Press 1986.
Mahar, William J.: Black English in Early Blackface Minstrelsy. A New Interpretation of the Sources of Minstrel Show Dialect. In: American Quarterly, 37, 1985, 2, pp. 260-285.
—: Behind the Burnt Cork Mask. Early Blackface Minstrelsy and Antebellum American Popular Culture. Urbana: University of Illinois Press 1999.
Manring, Maurice M. Slave in a Box. The Strange Career of Aunt Jemima. Charlottesville: University Press of Virginia 1998.
—: Aunt Jemima Explained. The Old South, the Absent Mistress, and the Slave in a Box. In: The Object Reader, ed. by Fiona Candlin and Raiford Guins. New York etc.: Routledge 2009, pp. 343-365.

Martin, Peter: Schwarze Teufel, Edle Mohren. Afrikaner in Geschichte und Bewußtsein der Deutschen. Hamburg: Junius 1993.

— and Alonzo, Christine (eds.): Zwischen Charleston und Stechschritt. Schwarze im Nationalsozialismus. Hamburg etc.: Dölling und Galitz 2004.

McClintock, Anne: Imperial Leather. Race, Gender and Sexuality in the Colonial Contest. New York etc.: Routledge 1995.

McElya, Micki: Clinging to Mammy. The Faithful Slave in Twentieth-Century America. Cambridge (Mass.) etc.: Harvard University Press 2007.

McEwan, Cheryl: Postcolonialism and Development. New York etc.: Routledge 2009.

Mehaffy, Marilyn M.: Advertising Race / Raceing Advertising. The Feminist Consumer (-Nation), 1876-1900. In: Signs, 23, 1997, 1, pp. 131-174.

Melzer, Annabelle: Spectacles and Sexualitites: The ›Mis-en-Scéne‹ of the ›Tirailleur Sénegalais‹ on the Western Front, 1914-1920. In: Borderlines. Genders and Identities in War and Peace, 1870-1930, ed. by Billie Melman. New York etc.: Routledge 1998, pp. 213-244.

Mendible, Myra: Embodying Latinidad. An Overview. In: From Bananas to Buttocks. The Latina Body in Popular Film and Culture, ed. by Myra Mendible. Austin: University of Texas Press 2007, pp. 1-28.

Menninger, Annerose: Die Verbreitung von Schokolade, Kaffee, Tee und Tabak in Europa (16. bis 19. Jahrhundert). Ein Vergleich. In: Berner Zeitschrift für Geschichte und Heimatkunde, 63, 2001, 1, pp. 28-37.

Merskin, Debra: The Princess and the SUV. Brand Images of Native Americans as Commodified Racism. In: Studies in Symbolic Interaction, Vol. 33, ed. by Norman K. Denzin. Bingley: Emerald 2009, pp. 129-148.

Michel, Marc: L'image du soldat noir. In: Images et Colonies. Iconographie et propagande coloniale sur l'Afrique française de 1880 à 1962, ed. by Nicolas Bancel, Pascal Blanchard and Laurent Gervereau. Paris: Bibliothèque de documentation internationale contemporaine 1993, pp. 86-91.

Miller, Daniel: Material Culture and Mass Consumption. Oxford etc.: Blackwell 1987.

Mills, Charles W.: The Racial Contract. Ithaca etc.: Cornell University Press 1997.

Mink, Gwendolyn: Meat vs. Rice (and Pasta). Samuel Gompers and the Republic of White Labor. In: Racially Writing the Republic. Racists, Race Rebels, and Transformations of American Identity, ed. by Bruce Baum and Duchess Harris. Durham etc.: Duke University Press 2009, pp.145-162.

Mintz, Sidney W., and Price, Richard: The Birth of African-American

Culture: An Anthropological Perspective. Boston: Beacon Press 1976.
—: Sweetness and Power. The Place of Sugar in Modern History. New York: Penguin 1985.
Montgomery, Elvin: Collecting African American History. A Celebration of America's Black Heritage through Documents, Artifacts, and Collectibles. New York etc.: Stewart 2001.
Moran III, Francis: Between Primates and Primitives. Natural Man as the Missing Link in Rousseau's Second Discourse. In: Philosophers on Race. Critical Essays, ed. by Julie K. Ward and Tommy L. Lott. Oxford etc.: Blackwell 2002, pp. 125-144.
Morgan, Jo-Ann: Mammy the Huckster. Selling the Old South for the New Century. In: American Art, 9, 1995, 1, pp. 86-109.
Morlang, Thomas: Askari und Fitafita. ›Farbige‹ Söldner in den deutschen Kolonien. Berlin: Ch. Links 2008.
Motley, Carol M., Henderson, Geraldine R., and Baker, Stacey M.: Exploring Collective Memories Associated with African-American Advertising Memorabilia. The Good, the Bad, and the Ugly. In: Journal of Advertising, 32, 2003, 1, pp. 47-57.
Nagl, Tobias: ›...und lass mich filmen und tanzen bloß um mein Brot zu verdienen‹. Schwarze Komparsen und Kinoöffentlichkeit in der Weimarer Republik. In: AfrikanerInnen in Deutschland und schwarze Deutsche – Geschichte und Gegenwart, ed. by Marianne Bechhaus-Gerst und Reinhard Klein-Arendt. Münster: Lit 2004, pp. 139-154.
Nederveen Pieterse, Jan: White on Black. Images of Africa and Blacks in Western Popular Culture. New Haven etc.:Yale University Press 1992.
Neely, Jr., Mark E.: The Boundaries of American Political Culture in the Civil War Era. Chapel Hill: University of North Carolina Press 2005.
Nelson, Keith L.: The ›Black Horror on the Rhine‹. Race as a Factor in Post-World War I Diplomacy. In: The Journal of Modern History, 42, 1970, 4, pp. 606-627.
Noble, Peter: The Negro in Films. London etc.: Skelton Robinson 1948.
Norton, Marcy: Sacred Gifts, Profane Pleasures. A History of Tobacco and Chocolate in the Atlantic World. Ithaca etc.: Cornell University Press 2008.
Nowatzki, Robert: Representing African Americans in Transatlantic Abolitionism and Blackface Minstrelsy. Baton Rouge: Louisiana State University Press 2010.
Nussbaum, Felicity A.: Between ›Oriental‹ and ›Blacks So Called‹. In: The Postcolonial Enlightenment. Eighteenth-Century Colonialism and Postcolonial Theory, ed. by Daniel Carey and Lynn Festa. Oxford etc.: Oxford University Press 2009, pp. 137-166.

Oguntoye, Katharina, Opitz, May, and Schultz, Dagmar (eds.): Farbe bekennen. Afro-deutsche Frauen auf den Spuren ihrer Geschichte. Berlin: Orlanda 1986.

Olupona, Jacob K.: A Tale of Two Germans and the Yoruba of Nigeria. Leo Frobenius (1873-1938) and Ulli Beier (*1922). In: European Traditions in the Study of Religion in Africa, ed. by Frieder Ludwig and Afe Adogame. Wiesbaden: Harrassowitz 2004, pp. 187-196.

O'Sullivan, Tim et al.: Key Concepts in Communication and Cultural Studies, 2nd ed. London etc.: Routledge 1994.

Owens, Erica, and Beistle, Bronwyn: Eating the Black Body. Interracial Desire, Food Metaphor and White Fear. In: Body/Embodiment. Symbolic Interactions and the Sociology of the Body, ed. by Dennis Waskul and Phillip Vannini. Aldershot etc.: Ashgate 2006, pp. 201-212.

Painter, Nell I.: The History of the White People. New York etc.: W. W. Norton 2010.

Parkin, Katherine J.: Food is Love. Food Advertising and Gender Roles in Modern America. Philadelphia: University of Pennsylvania Press 2006.

Paterson, Mark: Consumption and Everyday Life. New York etc.: Routledge 2006.

Patterson, James T.: Grand Expectations. The United States, 1945-1974. Oxford etc.: Oxford University Press 1996.

Patterson, Orlando: The Sociology of Slavery. An Analysis of the Origins, Development and Structure of Negro Slave Society in Jamaica. London etc.: MacGibbon & Kee 1967.

—: Slavery and Social Death. A Comparative Study. Cambridge (Mass.) etc.: Harvard University Press 1982.

Pearce, Susan M.: On Collecting. An Investigation into Collecting in the European Tradition. New York etc.: Routledge 1995.

Pederson, Jay P. (ed.): International Directory of Company Histories, Vol. 22. Detroit etc.: St. James 1998.

Perkins, Suzanne: Is It a Chocolate Pot? Chocolate and Its Accoutrements in France from Cookbook to Collectible. In: Chocolate. History, Culture, and Heritage, ed. by Louis E. Grivetti and Howard-Yana Shapiro. Hoboken: Wiley 2009, pp. 157-176.

Petroni, Frank A.: ›Uncle Toms‹. White Stereotypes in the Black Movement. In: Human Organization, 29, 1970, 4, pp. 260-266.

Philcox, Richard and Britton, Cecilia: Frantz Fanon. Retrieving a Lost Voice. In: Translation Review, 71, 2006, pp. 3-7.

Phillips, Ruth B., and Steiner, Christopher B.: Art, Authenticity, and the Baggage of Cultural Encounter. In: Unpacking Culture. Art and Commodity in Colonial and Postcolonial Worlds, ed. by Ruth B. Phillips and Christopher B. Steiner. Berkeley etc.: University of California

Press 1999, pp. 3-19.
Pickering, Michael: White Skin, Black Masks. ›Nigger‹ Minstrelsy in Victorian England. In: Music Hall: Performance and Style, ed. by Jacqueline S. Bratton. Milton Keynes etc.: Open University Press 1986, pp. 70-91.
—: Stereotyping. The Politics of Representation. Houndmills etc.: Palgrave 2001.
—: Racial Stereotypes. In: Social Identities. Multidisciplinary Approaches, ed. by Gary Taylor and Steve Spencer. New York etc.: Routledge 2004, pp. 91-106.
Pilgrim, David: The Picaninny Caricature. In: Jim Crow Museum of Racist Memorabilia, 2000, http://www.ferris.edu/jimcrow/picaninny/ [19.07.2010].
—: The Garbage Man. Why I Collect Racist Objects. In: Jim Crow Museum of Racist Memorabilia, 2005, http://www.ferris.edu/jimcrow/collect/ [07.09.2011].
Pipes, Daniel: Black Soldiers in Early Muslim Armies. In: The International Journal of African Historical Studies, 13, 1980, 1, pp. 87-94.
—: Slave Soldiers and Islam. The Genesis of a Military System. New Haven: Yale University Press 1981.
Pluchon, Pierre: Toussaint Louverture. Un révolutionnaire noir d'Ancien Régime, 2nd ed. Paris: École des loisirs 1989.
Polaschegg, Andrea: Der andere Orientalismus. Regeln deutsch-morgendländischer Imagination im 19. Jahrhundert. Berlin: W. De Gruyter 2004.
Price, Richard: Maroon Societies. Rebel Slave Communities in the Americas. Garden City: Anchor Press 1973.
Radano, Ronald: Hot Fantasies. American Modernism and the Idea of Black Rhythm. In: Music and the Racial Imagination, ed. by Ronald Radano and Philip V. Bohlman. Chicago etc.: University of Chicago Press 2000, pp. 459-480.
Ramamurthy, Anandi: Imperial Persuaders. Images of Africa and Asia in British Advertising. Manchester etc.: Manchester University Press 2003.
Reinders, Robert C.: Racialism on the Left. E.D. Morel and the ›Black Horror on the Rhine‹. In: International Review of Social History, 13, 1968, 1, pp. 1-28.
Reno, Dawn E.: The Encyclopedia of Black Collectibles. A Value and Identification Guide. Radnor: Wallace-Homestead 1995.
Reshef, Ouriel: Guerre, mythes et caricature. Au berceau d'une mentalité française. Paris: Presses de la Fondation nationale des sciences politiques 1984.
Rice, Alan: ›Who's Eating Whom‹. The Discourse of Cannibalism in the Literature of the Black Atlantic from Equitano's Travels to Toni Mor-

rison's Beloved. In: Research in African Literatures, 29, 1998, 4 , pp. 106-121.
—: Radical Narratives of the Black Atlantic. London etc.: Continuum 2003.
Rice, Laura: African Conscripts/European Conflicts. Race, Memory, and the Lessons of War. In: Cultural Critique, 45, 2000, pp. 109-149.
—: Of Irony and Empire. Islam, the West, and the Transcultural Invention of Africa. Albany: State University of New York Press 2007.
Richards, Thomas: The Commodity Culture of Victorian England. Advertising and Spectacle, 1851-1914. London: Verso 1991.
Richardson, David: Through African Eyes. The Middle Passage and the British Slave Trade. In: Representing Slavery. Art, Artefacts and Archives in the Collections of the National Maritime Museum, ed. by Douglas Hamilton and Robert Blyth. Aldershot etc.: Lund Humphries 2007, pp. 42-49.
Riesche, Barbara: Schöne Mohrinnen, edle Sklaven, schwarze Rächer. Schwarzendarstellungen und Sklavereithematik im deutschen Unterhaltungstheater (1770-1814), unpublished doctoral thesis. München: 2007.
Ringer, Benjamin B.: ›We the People‹ and Others: Duality and America's Treatment of its Racial Minorities. New York etc.: Tavistock 1983.
Robinson, John C., and Saúco, Victor G.: Bananas and Plantains. Wallingford etc.: CAB International 2010.
Roediger, David: The Wages of Whiteness. Race and the Making of the American Working Class. London etc.: Verso 1991.
Rosello, Mireille: Declining the Stereotype. Ethnicity and Representation in French Cultures. Hanover: University Press of New England 1998.
Rotberg, Robert I., and Rabb, Theodore K. (eds.): Art and History. Images and Their Meaning. Cambridge: Cambridge University Press 1988.
Rotman, Youval: Byzantine Slavery and the Mediterranean World, 1st eng. ed., transl. by Jane M. Todd. Cambridge (Mass.) etc.: Harvard University Press 2009.
Rudwick, Elliot M., and Meier, August: Black Man in the »White City«. Negroes and the Columbian Exposition, 1893. In: Phylon, 26, 1965, 4, pp. 354-361.
Ryan, Órla: Chocolate Nations. Living and Dying for Cocoa in West Africa. London etc.: Zed 2011.
Rydell, Robert W.: ›Darkest Africa‹. African Shows at America's World's Fairs, 1893-1940. In: Africans on Stage. Studies in Ethnological Show Business, ed. by Bernth Lindfors. Bloomington: Indiana University Press 1999, pp. 135-155.
Said, Edward: Orientalism, 4th ed. with a new afterword. London etc.:

Penguin 1995.
Sartre, Jean-Paul: Black Orpheus, transl. by John MacCombie. In: The Massachusetts Review, 6, 1964, 1, pp. 13-52.
Sauer, Walter: Stereotypen der österreichisch-afrikanischen Begegnung. In: Früchte der Zeit. Afrika, Diaspora, Literatur und Migration, ed. by Helmuth A. Niederle et al. Wien: WUV Universitätsverlag 2001, pp. 181-192.
Sauveurs des marques. In: Stratégies, 1291, 2003, http://www.strategies.fr/articles/r2999 6W/sauveurs-de-marques.html [27.08.2011].
Scheck, Raffael: Hitler's African Victims. The German Army Massacres of Black French Soldiers in 1940. Cambridge etc.: Cambridge University Press 2006.
Schiebinger, Londa: The Anatomy of Difference. Race and Sex in Eighteenth Century Science. In: Eighteenth-Century Studies, 23, 1990, 4, pp. 387-405.
Schneider, Dorothy, and Schneider, Carl J.: Slavery in America. New York: Facts on File 2007.
Schotland, Sara D.: Africans as Objects. Hogarth's Complex Portrayal of Exploitation. In: Journal of African American Studies, 13, 2009, 2, pp. 147-163.
Science. Richer Rice. In: Time, 28 June 1943, http://www.time.com/time/magazine/articl e/0,9171,790987,00.html [19.08.2011].
Segal, Ronald: Islam's Black Slaves. The History of Africa's Other Black Diaspora. London: Atlantic 2001.
Senghor, Leopold S. (ed.): Anthologie de la nouvelle poésie nègre et malgache de langue français. Paris: Presses Universitaires de France 1948.
—: Hosties noires, 1948. In: id., Poèmes. Paris: Éditions du Seuil 1971.
Sephocle, Marilyn: Anton Wilhelm Amo. In: Journal of Black Studies, 23, 1992, 2, pp. 182-187.
Shilliam, Robbie: A Fanonian Critique of Lebow's A Cultural Theory of International Relations. In: Millennium – Journal of International Studies, 38, 2009, pp. 117-136.
Shortridge, James R., and Shortridge, Barbara G.: Patterns of American Rice Consumption 1955 and 1980. In: Geographical Review, 73, 1983, 4, pp. 417-429.
Sieg, Katrin: Ethnic Drag. Performing Race, Nation, Sexuality in West Germany. Ann Arbor: University of Michigan Press 2002.
Silk, Catherine, and Silk, John: Racism and Anti-Racism in American Popular Culture. Portrayals of African-Americans in Fiction and Film. Manchester etc.: Manchester University Press 1990.
Smedley, Audrey: Race in North America. Origin and Evolution of a Worldview, 3rd ed. Boulder: Westview 2007.
Snowden, Jr., Frank M.: Before Color Prejudice. The Ancient View of

Blacks. Cambridge (Mass.) etc.: Harvard University Press 1983.
Sobich, Frank O.: »Schwarze Bestien, rote Gefahr«. Rassismus und Antisozialismus im deutschen Kaiserreich. Frankfurt a. M.: Campus 2006.
Solbrig, Ingeborg H.: American Slavery in Eighteenth-Century German Literature. The Case of Herder's ›Neger-Idyllen‹. In: Monatshefte, 82, 1990, 1, pp. 38-49.
Sombart, Werner: Luxury and Capitalism (1st German ed.: Leibzig etc.: 1913), transl. by W. R. Dittmar. Ann Arbor: University of Michigan Press 1967.
Sommerville, Diane M.: The Rape Myth in the Old South Reconsidered. In: The Journal of Southern History, 61, 1995, 3, pp. 481-518.
Solow, Barbara, and Engerman, Stanley L. (eds.): British Capitalism and Caribbean Slavery. The Legacy of Eric Williams. Cambridge etc.: Cambridge University Press 1987.
Springhall, John: The Genesis of Mass Culture. Show Business Live in America, 1840-1940. New York etc.: Palgrave Macmillan 2008.
Stampp, Kenneth M.: The Peculiar Institution. Slavery in the Ante-Bellum South. New York: Knopf 1956.
Stanonis, Anthony J.: Creating the Big Easy. New Orleans and the Emergence of Modern Tourism 1918-1945. Athens: University of Georgia Press 2006.
Staum, Martin S.: Labeling People. French Scholars on Society, Race, and Empire, 1815-1848. Montreal etc.: McGill-Queen's University Press 2003.
Stinchcombe, Arthur L.: Sugar Island Slavery in the Age of Enlightenment. The Political Economy of the Caribbean World. Princeton: Princeton University Press 1995.
Stowe, Harriet B.: Uncle Tom's Cabin (1st ed.: Boston etc.: 1852), republished by Elizabeth Ammons (ed.). New York etc.: Norton 1994.
Strausbaugh, John: Black Like You. Blackface, Whiteface, Insult & Imitation in American Popular Culture. New York: Jeremy P. Tarcher 2006.
Striker, Ardelle: Spectacle in the Service of Humanity. The Negrophile Play in France from 1789 to 1850. In: Black American Literature Forum, 19, 1985, 2, pp. 76-82.
Suckale-Redlefsen, Gude: Mauritius. Der heilige Mohr / The Black Saint Maurice. Houston: Menil Foundation 1987.
Sussman, Charlotte: Consuming Anxieties. Consumer Protest, Gender and British Slavery, 1713-1833. Stanford: Stanford University Press 2000.
Swisher, Margaret: Commercial Chocolate Posters. Reflections of Cultures, Values, and Times. In: Chocolate. History, Culture, and Heritage, ed. by Louis E. Grivetti and Howard-Yana Shapiro. Hoboken:

Wiley 2009, pp. 193-198.
Taguieff, Pierre-André: The Force of Prejudice. On Racism and Its Doubles, transl. by Hassan Melehy. Minneapolis etc.: University of Minnesota Press 2001.
Taylor, Gary: Buying Whiteness. Race, Culture, and Identity from Columbus to Hip Hop. New York etc.: Palgrave Macmillan 2005.
Terrio, Susan J.: Crafting the Culture and History of French Chocolate. Berkeley etc.: University of California Press 2000.
—: Chocolate. In: American Anthropologist, 105, 2003, 1, pp. 150-153.
Thode-Arora, Hilke: Afrika-Völkerschauen in Deutschland. In: AfrikanerInnen in Deutschland und schwarze Deutsche – Geschichte und Gegenwart, ed. by Marianne Bechhaus-Gerst and Reinhard Klein-Arendt. Münster etc.: Lit 2004, pp. 25-40.
Tobin, Beth F.: Picturing Imperial Power. Colonial Subjects in Eighteenth-Century British Painting. Durham etc.: Duke University Press 1999.
Tompkins, Kyla W.: Everything ›Cept Eat Us‹. The Antebellum Black Body Portrayed as Edible Body. In: Callaloo, 30, 2007, 1, pp. 201-224.
Trexler, Richard C.: The Journey of the Magi. Meanings in History of a Christian Story. Princeton etc.: Princeton University Press 1997.
Turner, Patricia A.: Ceramic Uncles & Celluloid Mammies. Black Images and Their Influence on Culture. New York etc.: Anchor 1994.
United States Holocaust Memorial Museum: The Nazi Olympics, Berlin 1936. The Facade of Hospitality. In: http://www.ushmm.org/museum/exhibit/online/olympics/detail.php?content=facade_hospitality [22.04.2011].
Uzgalis, William: ›An Inconsistency not to be Excused‹. On Locke and Racism. In: Philosophers on Race. Critical Essays, ed. by Julie K. Ward and Tommy L. Lott. Oxford etc.: Blackwell 2002, pp. 81-100.
Van Deburg, William L.: Slavery & Race in American Popular Culture. Madison etc.: University of Wisconsin Press 1984.
Van den Avenne, Cécile: Bambara et français-tirailleur. Une analyse de la politique linguistique de l'armée française: la Grande Guerre et après. In: Documents pour l'histoire du français langue étrangère ou seconde, 35, 2005, pp. 123-150.
Vaughan, Alden T.: From White Man to Redskin. Changing Anglo-American Perceptions of the American Indian. In: The American Historical Review, 87, 1982, 4, pp. 917-953.
Verkerk, Dorothy H.: Black Servant, Black Demon. Color Ideology in the Ashburnham Pentateuch. In: Journal of Medieval and Early Modern Studies, 31, 2001, 1, pp. 57-77.
Verney, Kevern: The Debate on Black Civil Rights in America. Manchester: Manchester University Press 2006.

Wallace-Sanders, Kimberly: Mammy. A Century of Race, Gender, and Southern Memory. Ann Arbor: University of Michigan Press 2008.

Ward, Julie K., and Lott, Tommy L. (eds.): Philosophers on Race. Critical Essays. Oxford etc.: Blackwell 2002.

Washington, Michele Y.: Ironic Authority. African American Images in Food Advertising. In: America I Am. Pass It Down Cookbook, ed. by Jeff Henderson and Ramin Ganeshram. New York: Tavis Smiley 2011, pp. 43-45.

Watson, Andrew: Agricultural Innovation in the Early Islamic World. The Diffusion of Crops and Farming Techniques, 700-1100. Cambridge etc.: Cambridge University Press 1983.

Weiß, Anja: Racist Symbolic Capital. A Bourdieuian Approach to the Analysis of Racism. In: Wages of Whiteness & Racist Symbolic Capital, ed. by Wulf D. Hund, Jeremy Krikler and David R. Roediger. Berlin etc.: Lit 2010, pp. 37-56.

Wengeler, Martin: Von der Hilfe für unterentwickelte Gebiete über den Neokolonialismus bis zur Entwicklungszusammenarbeit. Der sprachliche Umgang mit dem Nord-Süd Konflikt. In: Kontroverse Begriffe. Geschichte des öffentlichen Sprachgebrauchs in der Bundesrepublik Deutschland, ed. by Georg Stötzel und Martin Wengeler. Berlin: W. de Gruyter 1995, pp. 679-710.

Westbrook, Virginia: Role of Trade Cards in Marketing Chocolate During the Late 19th Century. In: Chocolate. History, Culture, and Heritage, ed. by Louis E. Grivetti and Howard-Yana Shapiro. Hoboken: Wiley 2009, pp. 183-192.

Wierlemann, Sabine: Political Correctness in den USA und in Deutschland. Berlin: Erich Schmidt 2002.

Wigger, Iris: »Die Schwarze Schmach am Rhein«. Rassistische Diskriminierung zwischen Geschlecht, Klasse, Nation und Rasse. Münster: Westfälisches Dampfboot 2007.

— and Klein, Katrin: ›Bruder Mohr‹. Angelo Soliman und der Rassismus der Aufklärung, In: Entfremdete Körper. Rassismus als Leichenschändung, ed. by Wulf D. Hund. Bielefeld: Transcript 2009, pp. 81-115.

—: ›Black Shame‹ – the campaign against ›racial degeneration‹ and female degradation in interwar Europe. In: Race & Class, 51, 2010, 3, pp. 33-46.

Williams, Eric E.: Capitalism & Slavery. Chapel Hill: University of North Carolina Press 1944.

Williamson, Judith: Decoding Advertisements. Ideology and Meaning in Advertising. London etc.: Boyars 1978.

Winn, J. Emmett: Documenting Racism in an Agricultural Extension Film. In: Film & History, 28, 2008, 1, pp. 33-43.

Wolter, Stefanie: Die Vermarktung des Fremden. Exotismus und die An-

fänge des Massenkonsums. Frankfurt etc.: Campus 2005.
Wood, Marcus: Blind Memory. Visual Representations of Slavery in England and America 1780-1865. Manchester etc.: Manchester University Press 2000.
—: Slavery, Empathy and Pornography. Oxford etc.: Oxford University Press 2002.
Wood, Peter H.: Black Majority. Negroes in Colonial South Carolina from 1670 through the Stono Rebellion. New York etc.: Norton 1974.
Wray, Matt: Not Quite White. White Thrash and the Boundaries of Whiteness. Durham etc.: Duke University Press 2006.
Y'a bon Banania ou Y'a pas bon Banania. In: Congopage blog, 6 October 2005, http://w ww.congopage.com/Y-a-bon-Banania-ou-Y-a-pas-bon [10.09.2011].
›Y'a bon Banania‹ disparaîtra bel et bien. In: L'Express, 20 May 2011, http://www.lexpress.fr/styles/minute-saveurs/y-a-bon-banania-disparaitra-bel-et-bien _994798.html [10.09.2011].
Young, Robert J. C.: Colonial Desire. Hybridity in Theory, Culture and Race. New York etc.: Routledge 1995.
Zeller, Joachim: Der magische Sarotti-Mohr. Rezension von: Der Sarotti Mohr. Die bewegte Geschichte einer Werbefigur. In: iz3w, 283, 2005, p. 28.
— and Wegmann, Heiko: ›Mohren‹ – Ein Stereotyp in der Alltagskultur. In: Freiburg Postkolonial, 2008, http://www.freiburg-postkolonial.de /Seiten/Mohren-Stereotyp.htm [07.07.2011].
—: Bilderschule der Herrenmenschen. Koloniale Reklamesammelbilder. Berlin: Ch. Links 2008.
—: Harmless Kolonialbiedermeier? Colonial and Exotic Trading Cards. In: German Colonialism, Visual Culture, and Modern Memory, ed. by Volker M. Langbehn. New York etc.: Routledge 2010, pp. 71-86.
Zimmerman, Andrew: Anthropology and Antihumanism in Imperial Germany. Chicago etc.: The University of Chicago Press 2001.